Teacher
Education
and Autism

by the same author

Asperger Syndrome
What Teachers Need to Know
Second Edition
Matt Winter with Clare Lawrence
ISBN 978 1 84905 203 0
eISBN 978 0 85700 430 7

Autism and Flexischooling
A Shared Classroom and Homeschooling Approach
Clare Lawrence
ISBN 978 1 84905 279 5
eISBN 978 0 85700 582 3

**Successful School Change and Transition
for the Child with Asperger Syndrome**
A Guide for Parents
Clare Lawrence
ISBN 978 1 84905 052 4
eISBN 978 0 85700 358 4

How to Make School Make Sense
A Parents' Guide to Helping the
Child with Asperger Syndrome
Clare Lawrence
ISBN 978 1 84310 664 7
eISBN 978 1 84642 834 0

of related interest

The Neurodiverse Classroom
A Teacher's Guide to Individual Learning
Needs and How to Meet Them
Victoria Honeybourne
ISBN 978 1 78592 362 3
eISBN 978 1 78450 703 9

**The Essential Manual for Asperger
Syndrome (ASD) in the Classroom**
What Every Teacher Needs to Know
Kathy Hoopmann
Illustrated by Rebecca Houkamau
ISBN 978 1 84905 553 6
eISBN 978 0 85700 984 5

Teacher Education and Autism

A Research-Based Practical Handbook

Edited by *Clare Lawrence*
Foreword by *Tony Attwood*

Jessica Kingsley *Publishers*
London and Philadelphia

Additional resources are available to download from www.jkp.com/catalogue/book/ 9781785926044. These can be downloaded for personal use with this program, but may not be reproduced for any other purposes without the permission of the publisher.

First published in 2019
by Jessica Kingsley Publishers
73 Collier Street
London N1 9BE, UK
and
400 Market Street, Suite 400
Philadelphia, PA 19106, USA

www.jkp.com

Library of Congress Cataloging in Publication Data
A CIP catalog record for this book is available from the Library of Congress

British Library Cataloguing in Publication Data
A CIP catalogue record for this book is available from the British Library

ISBN 978 1 78592 604 4
eISBN 978 1 78592 608 2

Printed and bound in Great Britain

Contents

Foreword

We now recognise that autism occurs much more frequently than we originally thought. Thus, it could be anticipated that every other class will have at least one child who has autism. Teacher training, therefore, needs to provide education and guidance on how to accommodate the characteristics of autism in the classroom and during the school day.

The characteristics of autism can be summarised as a different way of perceiving, thinking, learning and relating: not necessarily defective, but different. Typical children are the overwhelming majority in a classroom, and the curriculum may be presented in a social and conversational style that suits their profile of abilities. However, children who have autism have difficulties with the social and conversational aspects of life. Conventional teaching styles can cause considerable stress and confusion and may even inhibit learning. I have asked many children with autism, 'What do you admire in a teacher?' The replies have been illuminating, and include comments such as:

A teacher who:

- knows how I think and what motivates me

- is calm and reassuring, especially when I am confused or experiencing a meltdown

- does not make me feel stupid

- controls the other students so that I feel safe and can concentrate

- knows when I need to take a break

- is prepared to make an exception

- helps me organise what I need in class and for homework

- helps prepare me for changes, especially the unexpected

- ensures the other students follow the school rules

- has a sense of humour

- knows and accepts when I need to be alone

- gives me time and is patient when I am trying to explain something

- understands my perspective and experiences.

Some teachers are intuitively able to understand autism and quickly develop a rapport, while others need to have an open mind and learn how to create an autism-friendly classroom and school. This valuable handbook will provide guidance in how a child who has autism is different to their peers and how a teacher can understand and accommodate these differences to ensure that school provides the opportunity to learn both the academic and social curriculum.

Tony Attwood

Acknowledgements

I would like to thank the contributors to this book, each of whom has shared their expertise and enthusiasm, and who together have produced a resource that is rich, varied and original. They have not been afraid to ask questions or to think 'outside the box', and their various responses to the autism conundrum have greatly deepened my own understanding. Thank you, one and all!

A Word about Language

Terminology around autism is a minefield. As of DSM-5 in 2013 and ICD-11 in 2018, Asperger syndrome has ceased to exist as a diagnosis, yet many people (and these are people with a diagnosed issue with change) were given this diagnosis and wish to continue to use it. In diagnostic criteria Asperger syndrome has been subsumed into the wider diagnosis of autism spectrum disorder (ASD), yet this term has issues of its own. Some find the concept of a 'spectrum' challenging, given its implication of a range of autism that is (I believe wrongly) implied to span from mild to severe, and many others have issue with the wholly negative word 'disorder'. Some have taken ASD to stand for autism spectrum difference instead, and others prefer ASC, standing for autism spectrum condition. Meanwhile, the American Psychological Association (APA), who are largely the arbiters of academic writing style, still suggests the use of 'person-first' language, that is, 'person with autism' or 'person with a disorder on the autism spectrum'. These phrases hardly roll off the tongue.

Research by Kenny *et al.* (2016) suggests a way out of this difficulty. This research sought language use preferences around autism, and – although it did not find universal agreement – the term preferred by autistic people themselves and their families was 'autistic'. In response, the National Autistic Society now advocates for increased use of the term autistic, and that is the term that is usually used in this book.

Reference

Kenny, L., Hattersley, C., Molins, B., Buckley, C., Povey, C. and Pellicano, E. (2016) Which terms should be used to describe autism? Perspectives from the UK autism community. *Autism 20,* 4, 442–462.

INTRODUCTION

As of the academic year 2017/2018, autism education is a required element in Initial Teacher Education (ITE). This is, of course, excellent news for all of us trying to increase understanding of the perplexing and fascinating conundrum that is autism. If all newly qualified teachers enter the profession with better understanding of how to meet the needs of the autistic pupils in their classes, then this has got to be a great step forward.

Unfortunately, ITE is very squeezed. There are many, many elements to fit into the course, an initial course which – when postgraduate – may last for as little as ten months. In this context, elements of autism education may be very restricted. Often autism understanding is squeezed in between attention deficit hyperactivity disorder (ADHD) and dyslexia, and we may be lucky if it merits more than 90 minutes or so of a course.

But what if that is not the case? What if we take the time to educate our new teachers fully in the many ways that autism will affect our pupils? In this context, what would we want our new teachers to learn and think about?

This book attempts to answer these questions. It aims to be a cornucopia of interesting angles on autism and how autism might be considered in schools and classrooms. Each chapter contains the material for a session to be delivered to trainee teachers (or to currently working teachers through continuing professional development

(CPD)), or to provide a unit of self-study. Each chapter challenges us to reconsider autism within different educational contexts. There is a rich variety of contributors – some expert in primary education and some in secondary – and each has used this opportunity to present an angle on autism that they believe to be important. Each is essential: primary pupils with autism grow into secondary pupils, and secondary pupils grow from primary pupils. Continuity and consistency between education levels are key.

Many of the chapters contain tasks and points for discussion. There are also additional resources available to download at www.jkp.com/catalogue/book/9781785926044. Each of the subjects discussed in these chapters has wider educational implications, and each is valid ITE in its own right. Perhaps, with these subjects available to teacher educators, they may begin to become core content in teacher education as we begin to incorporate 'the autism angle' more centrally within wider education debate.

I hope you enjoy using this book. I am keen to hear feedback on the effectiveness of these chapters and would be delighted to receive your comments and suggestions at any time. Please do feel free to get in touch.

Clare Lawrence
Clarelawrence101@gmail.com

Chapter One

UNDERSTANDING AUTISM

Clare Lawrence

Autism is 'the name given to a behaviour pattern, produced in a complicated way, as the end result of a long chain of causation and there is no way of explaining it in a few words' (Wing, 1990/2013, p.1). This complexity is, I think, one reason why it is so perplexing to teachers. Autism can manifest itself in so many different ways, in different children and in the same child on different days or even at different times of day. Given this huge variety it can be difficult to even begin to formulate a plan to meet autistic pupils' needs. 'Differentiation for autism' simply cannot exist across the board.

Task 1.1

Discuss and describe autistic behaviours you have observed in pupils at school. What are 'autistic behaviours'? How would you expect a pupil diagnosed as autistic to present in the classroom?

There are signposts to understanding autism. The DSM-5 (APA, 2013) and ICD-11 (WHO, 2018) definition of autism is, in summary, that it is a persistent deficit in social communication and social interaction together with a restricted, repetitive pattern of behaviour, interests or activities.

Persistent deficits in social communication and social interaction

Social communication is the way that we that communicate with each other as people. This includes language and also non-verbal communication such as gesture, facial expression and tone of voice. An autistic pupil may struggle to understand what is meant rather than what is said (which are often not the same things) and may take language literally and have difficulty interpreting idioms or sarcasm. Some autistic pupils do not find spoken language an effective way to communicate but may prefer symbols, signing or the written word. It is important to bear in mind that pupils may understand either more or less than they appear to, and that communication is a two-way process. It is both expressed and received, and in either you may need to reconsider your communication method.

When social communication breaks down or is ineffective (which can be seen to be a communication deficit on either side of the interaction), it makes social interaction very challenging. An autistic person may have difficulty recognising or understanding the other person's feelings and intentions and may not be able to express their own effectively.

Restricted, repetitive patterns of behaviour, interests or activities

When social communication is difficult to read, the world can seem an unpredictable and confusing place. Many autistic people may seek to overcome this by establishing routines that work and can be depended upon. These can be hugely reassuring, and schools can use these effectively to support autistic pupils. However, they can also be the source of distress when these routines change. There may be a different teacher, the seating plan for the room may have altered or the predicted literature lesson may be changed at the last minute to a language one. These 'small' changes that are accommodated by most pupils can be the source of great anxiety for autistic pupils.

In the same way, other pupils not adhering to school rules can be very upsetting. Rules are likely to be reassuring for autistic pupils: they make the confusion of 'how to behave' so much clearer. Other pupils not abiding by these rules, or challenging the teacher, may be very alarming, as can a teacher who is non-specifically angry. A statement such as, 'I'm very angry with you; you are in big trouble', said non-specifically without a name attached, can be devastating for the autistic pupil.

A further feature of many autistic people's lives is their intense, highly-focused interests. These 'special interests' may vary but are often a source of great comfort and enjoyment for that individual. They are also an excellent 'place' for the autistic pupil to go to de-stress and can be a very practical way for the pupil to look after themselves. For example, if an autistic pupil is enabled to spend breaktime reading manga comics in the library, then that time is more likely to genuinely constitute a 'break' than if required to go outside and socialise.

Task 1.2

Look back at the examples you gave at the opening of the chapter. Do the diagnostic criteria describe these pupils? Are the criteria helpful in understanding what autism 'is'?

Understanding the autistic world

There are a number of theories of autism that have been suggested by academics to help understand the autistic world. These include theory of mind, weak central coherence, executive functioning and, importantly, sensory understanding.

Sensory understanding

In the last ten years or so we have become much more aware of the importance of sensory processing within autism. An autistic person may be either over sensitive (hyper-sensitive) or under sensitive (hypo-sensitive) to sensory input, whether that be sounds, touch, tastes, smells, light, colours or temperatures in the environment. They may also react unusually to internal sensations such as pain, balance, hunger, thirst or the need to empty bladder or bowels. For all of us, our understanding of the world arrives at our brains through our senses, and for autistic pupils they may literally inhabit a different world to those around them.

A while ago I was visiting a school to observe a trainee teacher. She had reported to me that the regular class teacher had warned her that these Year 9s were particularly lively. On some occasions, she had been told, they were giggly and restless one minute, then quiet the next, with their behaviour apparently synchronised. Their teacher could not explain it. The class teacher, like me, was in her 50s. Neither of us had any idea of what was going on. However, the trainee teacher was in her 20s and was able to identify the issue immediately. One of the pupils had an app on his phone which was emitting a high-pitched whistle, too high for our older ears to detect. The pupils could all hear it and found it hilarious. It took the young ears of the trainee to spot their ruse. This is an example of where different individuals occupy the same space but share different sensory experiences. Just because something is not real for us does not mean that it is not real. For children with autism, different perceptions of the sensory world may be experienced all the time.

Confusingly, no two children with autism will experience the same sensory differences, and the same child may experience different sensory differences at different times or on different days. What can be tolerated one day may be overwhelming the next. It is essential that as teachers we are sensitive to these sensory issues, rather than being distracted by responding to the behaviours – avoidant, anxious, self-injurious – which the sensory overload may prompt.

Equally, we need to be aware of the dangers of under sensitivity to sensory stimuli experienced by some children with autism. The child may not register pain, for example, nor be aware of extremes of heat and cold. Clearly, if these children are going to be in a position to learn, their sensory needs need to be addressed first.

The autistic child's sensory environment may seem strange to those who do not share it, and for some it may seem challenging. However, it is also a gift. Those who have the most heightened sensory acuity are revered by society – the top perfumiers, the chocolatier, the musician who hears the finest nuances of a piece or the conductor who follows each part within a symphony. I would argue that we need to accept and nurture the sensory differences of our autistic pupils, rather than focusing on de-sensitisation. Their sensitivities may be difficult for them to manage as children but may be nurtured into outstanding skills as adults.

Theory of mind

Theory of mind (ToM) was first expressed as a way of understanding autism in the 1980s (Baron-Cohen, Leslie and Frith, 1985). Theory of mind is about understanding that another person does not share the inner world of your mind. They do not know what you are thinking, and they may be thinking something totally different from you.

This can cause confusion when the autistic pupil makes assumptions about what you mean. You may say, 'I'm going to tell you all about the Romans.' What you mean is that you are going to spend some minutes telling the class some information about the Romans, but the autistic child may be alarmed (or intrigued) about the promise you have apparently made (and which you then break). Equally, you may fail in your ToM understanding of the pupil when, for example, you fail to realise that they have earache if they do not tell you that this is the case.

Difficulty with ToM can lead to many of the more visible characteristics of autism. However, teachers should never assume that pupils who appear not to have difficulty with ToM are without challenge. Recent research (Livingston *et al.*, 2018) suggests that autistic people who appear to exhibit more effective ToM have rather developed compensatory behaviour patterns whilst retaining the core cognitive challenge. In the research it was found that these so-called 'high compensators' also have higher levels of self-reported anxiety. This understanding is important for teachers, as it is imperative that we do not make assumptions about autistic pupils. Someone who does not apparently present with what we see as autistic behaviours may be working very hard to compensate for their ToM challenges, at the price of increased anxiety and stress. This 'masking' of autistic characteristics is explored further in Chapter Three.

Central coherence

This theory, originally articulated by Frith and Happé (1994), suggests that autistic people may have a local rather than a global processing bias. In other words, they may be focusing on the detail at the expense of seeing the larger picture – seeing the trees rather than the wood.

Although this is presented as a deficit (it is described as having weak central coherence), it can equally be a strength in some ways. One of the joys of teaching autistic pupils is the way that they may have the ability to notice detail, and to suggest theories and connections that you would not otherwise have made. It can lead to intense appreciation of smaller detail – of music, of language or visually – even if the larger implications of what is being studied may be missed. It is important to remember when teaching that the pupil may not be focusing on what you want them to focus on, but equally they may have a different and unusual focus that you have never considered. As with so much, it is always better to use the difference and to celebrate it, rather than to crush it or dismiss it.

Executive functioning

Executive functioning is what allows us the skills to know what to do and in what order, what to do first, when something is more important, and when something is finished. It allows us to multi-task, to prioritise, to predict and to estimate. I know that I can break two eggs into a saucepan of water on the hob, switch on the kettle, put two slices of bread into the toaster, pour the now boiling water onto tea-bags, transfer the toast to plates, spread it with butter, remove the tea-bags from the mugs and add milk to the tea...and lift two perfect poached eggs onto the toast for breakfast with my son, Sam. I can do this while listening to the radio and – frequently – texting on my phone. When Sam, who is autistic, makes us tea he boils the kettle, pours the water onto one tea-bag, waits for the tea to brew, removes the tea-bag, adds milk and brings me the cup. He then repeats the whole process from switching on the kettle for his own cup of tea. He finds my multi-tasking confusing and – at times – distressing. I find his single-minded focusing interesting and – because it is him – charming. I am simply grateful that he has learned that, when he wants a cup of tea, it may be possible that I would like one too. That is not a small achievement in autism.

Task 1.3

Do these theories of autism help in your understanding of the autistic behaviours you described at the beginning of this chapter? In what ways do they help you to understand that autism is not behaviour? Give examples of when school may be challenging for an autistic pupil with no visible behaviours present. How can you as that child's teacher be alert to these challenges?

References

APA (American Psychiatric Association) (2013) *Diagnostic and Statistical Manual of Mental Disorders (DSM-5)*. Washington, DC: American Psychiatric Association Publishing.

Baron-Cohen, S., Leslie, A.M. and Frith, U. (1985) Does the autistic child have a 'theory of mind'? *Cognition 21*, 1, 37–46.

Frith, U. and Happé, F. (1994) Autism: Beyond 'theory of mind'. *Cognition 50*, 1–3, 115–132.

Livingston, L.A., Colvert, E., Social Relationships Study Team, Bolton, P. and Happé, F. (2018) Good social skills despite poor theory of mind: Exploring compensation in autism spectrum disorder. *Journal of Child Psychology and Psychiatry*. doi: 10.1111/jcpp.12886

Wing, L. (1990/2013) 'What is Autism?' In K. Ellis (ed.) *Autism: Professional Perspectives and Practice*. New York: Springer.

World Health Organization (WHO) (2018) *The ICD-11 Classification of Mental and Behavioural Disorders: Clinical Descriptions and Diagnostic Guidelines*. Geneva: World Health Organization.

Chapter Two

THE AUTISTIC TEACHER

'Greg'

One 'voice' that is seldom heard around the issue of autism and education is that of the autistic teacher as there has been very little research into this perspective. 'Greg' – which is a pseudonym – is a trainee teacher on a postgraduate certificate in education (PGCE) course. His degree is in geography and education. He worked for some years as a teaching assistant (TA), and he is now training to become a secondary geography teacher. Greg is autistic, and here he shares some of his thoughts about becoming a teacher who has autism, and the insight that his own autism has given him into the needs of autistic pupils in school.

Each section gives some thoughts and opinions in Greg's voice and is followed by a task providing an opportunity to discuss questions that the extract raises. Each section/small group discussion should last approximately five to ten minutes of an hour's training session, allowing whole-group feedback on issues that have surfaced at the end.

It is worth noting that within any group of trainee teachers there could be any number who are autistic and who may or may not wish to share this identity.

Greg: I was very fortunate, as the teachers at my schools when I was a pupil were incredibly understanding and supportive. I know now that my experience is not what is had by all pupils with autism. I'm also fortunate because I've been able to learn about my own autism through my experience as a special needs TA, and by attending all sorts of autism training courses. This has really helped my understanding, so that I see autism not just from the personal perspective but through understanding of the theories too. These also give me credibility: I do know what I'm talking about...and I've got the certificates to prove it! This combination of personal and professional experience, coupled with training, puts me in a strong position to understand the needs of the autistic pupils I will teach.

Task 2.1

What is the ideal balance between personal experience, professional experience and theory in autism? Greg clearly values the opportunities he has had to learn about autism, rather than simply to 'live' it. Should we be providing autism understanding in school, both for autistic pupils and for their neurotypical peers? Where might this fit into the curriculum?

Greg: I am going to disclose my autism when I become teacher. It will mean that I can be a role model for autistic pupils. I'm not going to disclose it on the first day; it doesn't define me – it's more a quirk – but I'd like people to know.

Task 2.2

Think about the issues around a teacher's disclosure of an autism diagnosis. In what ways might disclosure have a positive or negative effect on the pupils, parents and staff? In what ways might it have a positive or negative effect on that individual teacher?

Greg: I believe that my autism is an asset in some elements of teaching. It gives me an eye for detail and a clarity – a 'black or white' approach which doesn't lead to ambiguity. It will also make me sensitive to the needs of autistic pupils in my classes and means that I will do the best I can to allow for their needs, although I also know that there are limits to the adjustment that can be achieved practically. Perhaps as well as being more sensitive to autistic pupils, I may also have the confidence to be more 'tough' with them. I think that building resilience in students with autism should be a big part of what we do. After all, there isn't always going to be someone there to hold their hand.

Task 2.3

In what other ways might being autistic be a strength in a teacher? How might it be a challenge?

Greg touches on the subject of differentiation for needs vs the need for pupils with difficulties – ultimately – to fit into the system. Where do you think this balance should lie? How much should adjustment be offset against a need to build resilience?

To what extent should the school make 'reasonable adjustment' to allow for Greg's autism, and what might this look like?

Greg: I feel that what is really important is that the various professionals in schools work together to meet the needs of autistic pupils, and to show each other mutual respect. It's also really important to keep parents involved. Parents don't always understand how schools work, but they are the ones who know that child best and it is important to treat them with respect and to value the insight into the wider picture of the child's life that they can bring. Parents can sometimes help to put the pupil's point of view forward if they are struggling to communicate. It is important for autistic pupils that their ideas and views should be heard within their own educational context.

Task 2.4

Greg mentions the importance of 'collaborative care' for autistic pupils, where professionals and parents work together for the good of the child. How – practically – can this be better achieved? He also suggests that the views of the autistic child should be heard. How can this 'voice' be added into the mix?

Greg: What's most important, though, is that the autistic child is happy at school. We should make the school experience as enjoyable as possible, and avoid the unhappiness, stress, fear and frustration that so many autistic pupils experience. The pupil's ideas and views need to be listened to and taken seriously. I also think it's important for autistic pupils to have a chance to learn about their own autism and what it means for them. That is just as important as exam results – although that said, we shouldn't have lower expectations of autistic pupils' academic potential just because of their autism. Just because someone may learn differently doesn't mean that they learn less well.

Task 2.5

Do you agree with Greg that the most important thing is that autistic pupils are happy? What are the arguments for and against this position?

What do you feel about 'setting' autistic pupils into lower ability groups? Is there any justification for it? If a child 'learns differently', how is that going to impact – positively or negatively – on the wider learning of the class?

Greg: I would very much like to bring greater autism understanding into the schools that I teach at, although schools mustn't have just one 'autism expert'. All staff should have an understanding of autism as a matter of course.

Task 2.6

What are the pros and cons of having a person with a difference providing training and support in school regarding that difference?

Chapter Three

AUTISM, MASKING, SOCIAL ANXIETY AND THE CLASSROOM

Luke Beardon

This chapter introduces you to the concepts of 'masking', and 'social anxiety'. It provides some rationale and potential explanations behind the concepts, offers links to some YouTube video clips that you should find useful, and gives some hints and tips as to what you as a teacher might be able to do to support your autistic learners.

First off, I must bring your attention to what I refer to as 'The Golden Equation'. Namely:

$$Autism + Environment = Outcome$$

What this means is that autism in and of itself will not (necessarily) impact on the person, at least not in a way in which you will automatically be able to understand or support the child without additional information; it is usually a mixture of the person and their environment that leads to the outcome for the autistic pupil. The outcome can be anything – on a scale of desperation to one of absolute contentment. If it can be accepted that one cannot change a person's autism (and this *is* something that should be accepted as fact) then the most effective way in which schools can be supportive is to change the environment. The 'environment' in this case is a combination of:

- the physical environment

- people

- products/ objects.

The physical environment will impact on the sensory needs of the person; this is outside the scope of this chapter, but the following link to a Blog entry of mine might be useful.[1] The people component is exactly that: any person within the vicinity could be impacting on the autistic individual, positively or negatively. And the 'products/ objects' are those things that form part of the environment but don't fit into the other two categories – mobile phones, for example.

This chapter will focus on the relationship between people and autistic social anxiety. Before I go any further, I should make a note about what I mean in terms of social anxiety. The 'social' bit probably speaks for itself – though it might need some clarification. Social essentially means contact with other people, but this contact could be anything ranging from email or text contact, through to having to follow a teacher's instruction, through to over-hearing a conversation on the other side of the classroom. It is anything and everything as regards spoken and written word, unwritten rules, non-verbal cues, body language, facial gesture – the autistic person has to cope with this entire gamut of interactions. The key difference here between the autistic person and the predominant neurotype (PNT) is that almost all of the aforementioned social contact will get processed in the *subconscious* part of the PNT brain. The autistic person, on the other hand, may have to (try to) make sense of any or all of it in the

---

1   https://blogs.shu.ac.uk/autism/2015/10/01/sensory-framework

conscious part of the brain – which can be, literally, overwhelming, or even impossible. What this does mean is that the level of anxiety for the autistic pupil having to try to figure out what on earth is going on around them in a social sense can be intense.

So, why is social contact such a stress? I have answered this in part above, noting that having to figure out social interactions at a conscious level can be exhausting – but take into account the following too; imagine that you:

1. have no access to unwritten rules of social engagement

2. don't know who you should be listening to, or why

3. following (2) don't know who you should be responding to

4. don't know how to respond

5. cannot order social contact in scales of importance

6. cannot understand the facial expressions that go with the words

7. cannot ascertain whether implied meaning is real or not

8. don't know whether instructions are trustworthy

9. find lies utterly distressing.

OK – to illustrate, these are very simple (but very real) examples of each of the above from an autistic perspective just based on one event:

1. Have no access to unwritten rules of social engagement

So I've gone into the assembly hall, and there are tons of people around. Some are sitting, some standing, some kind of lounging, some talking, some listening to phones, some on their own, some in groups, some in pairs, some laughing and joking, some who don't look happy at all – none of them look in a panic, which is what I am – how can so many people be doing so many different things, and all of them 'naturally' knowing what to do and how to do it? I haven't a clue, I just want to disappear.

2. Don't know who you should be listening to, or why

And there are literally dozens of conversations around me. Are any directed at me? Are all of them directed at me? Some people glance at me, some stare directly at me, some don't look my way – who is talking to me? Help!

3. Following (2) don't know who you should be responding to

I know if I don't respond when people speak to me I get told off, it happens all the time. And yet when I do respond, and it's to the wrong person, or to the wrong bit of conversation, then I get told I'm in the wrong. I'm in a no win situation yet again. The panic is beginning to grip harder.

4. Don't know how to respond

OK, so I think that girl has asked how I am doing today. I know what the question means, so that's good. But all I can think of is screaming at her, telling her that I'm about to burst into tears, wet myself, collapse into a heap, whack my head against the wall, or possibly all of the above simply to do anything – *anything* – to get out of this awful situation. But I also know that this kind of response is not what she is looking for.

5. Cannot order social contact in scales of importance

The teacher is standing on the stage. But that girl is still looking at me. Do I try and formulate an answer to her question – after all, it seems like it was a kind question; or do I shut up and sit down to wait for the teacher to speak? These decisions are just so overwhelming. I would happily have a heart attack, just to get me out of this situation.

6. Cannot understand the facial expressions that go with the words

She's asked me the question again, but this time her face has a totally different expression. Now I'm getting lost in studying her face trying to compare it to the expression that was on it previously. Why does she look different? What does the difference mean? My mind is filling up with all the different possibilities!

7. Cannot ascertain whether implied meaning is real or not

OK, she's now said, 'Oh, it doesn't matter, forget it...' – but do I really forget it? This question will now haunt me for days. I will spend hours going over the last three minutes, trying to work out what I could/ should have done. I will consider all eventualities, permutations and possible responses. And yet I will be none the wiser, and even more terrified the next time something similar happens.

8. Don't know whether instructions are trustworthy

The teacher has finally spoken. He's told us that it's important that we sit down, and there will be action taken if we don't sit immediately. But how important can it be? Lots of other kids are still stood up, and there doesn't seem to be any repercussion. I reckon it isn't really that important, but what do I know?

9. Find lies utterly distressing

The teacher has now said it's important that we understand the boundaries for personal space. But he also said there would be actions against those who didn't sit down straight away. I know for a fact that the latter wasn't true – should I believe him in this instance or not? My anxiety over what to believe and what not to is just too much. Along with the social interactions prior to Sir talking and lying, I have had enough of school, I feel a meltdown coming on.

School start time: 9.15 a.m.

Autistic meltdown: 9.25 a.m.

The above is just one isolated incident – but understanding it from the autistic perspective can be extremely illuminating. It becomes so much easier to understand why social anxiety exists. For each of the nine points illustrated, there are dozens more that could impact on the autistic pupil in school. Consider what the outcome might have been if the person had been told by a trusted staff member prior to assembly: 'Your instructions are to wait outside the hall until you hear Sir instruct everyone to sit down. Then enter the hall, sit down, and you don't need to speak with anyone. If, throughout the assembly, Sir or anyone else says something that you don't understand, write it down and we will discuss it afterwards.'

The autistic community have coined the term 'social hangover', which is a superb way of describing how too much social contact can lead to huge problems. Some of these have already been highlighted – but each autistic person will have their triggers. What is vital to remember is that social hangovers are very real, and should be avoided if at all possible.

One of the ways in which autistic people, including pupils within a school environment, learn to cope with social anxiety is to mask it – and this is often done by copying other children. Also known as camouflaging and mimicking, autistic individuals do this in order to not stand out or be the odd one out.[2]

---

2   The following clips could give a useful insight into this kind of 'behaviour':
    www.youtube.com/watch?v=2gOZFK9H5dQ
    www.youtube.com/watch?v=m5WURWkDL68
    www.youtube.com/watch?v=ps8lqMKXV1o

While much of what is said in the literature and in these clips refers to girls/women, boys/men can also mask and face very similar issues. Essentially, masking can on the one hand be an excellent way of getting through the day – but, on the other, it comes at a price. Having to mask constantly is not only utterly draining, it takes a huge amount of intellectual effort, which can have major implications at school, one's brain is being relied on to learn. For many autistic students, their actual learning ability is compromised by the effort taken up by masking.

Masking could be seen as a 'triple whammy':

1. brain drain

2. appearance of being fine

3. no one believes the parent.

So – brain drain having been covered – what about the latter two? A perennial issue that so often comes up in parent forums and discussions is that of school simply not believing the child or parent when they suggest that school is so anxiety inducing. The reason behind the denial is easy to understand – after all, the child 'appears' to be absolutely fine while at school. The irony of this is that the exact reason behind why they appear to be so fine is also one of the main reasons why they are so stressed – that is, having to focus so hard on their presentation of mimicking all the time. In such cases, many children 'behave' impeccably at school, and in essence 'save up' the social hangover consequences for the safety of their own home; and yet parents are frequently not believed when they suggest that their child is struggling at school – often, it is the quiet autistic child who might be in the greatest distress – and in need of understanding and support.

One last issue that is worth noting is that of the long-term implications of masking. While it might be an apparent useful 'tool' on a day-to-day basis, the long-term suppression of a 'true self' can have major implications for anyone's mental well-being.

Task

Ask yourself the following questions – if *any* response is a negative, then you may not be doing enough for your autistic students:

1. Do you know who all of your autistic students are?

2. Have you ensured that they are as protected as possible from social interaction should they wish to avoid it?

3. Is there space and time for your autistic students to access if they need to be on their own at any time during the day?

4. Do you have ongoing and positive two-way communication with your autistic students' parents/carers?

5. Are you aware of the possible ways in which your autistic students might mask their behaviour?

6. Do your autistic students have a single, trusted, named staff member to whom they can have access at times they need it?

7. Do you have a good understanding of what causes each of your autistic students anxiety?

8. Are you familiar with all of the signs that might indicate increased anxiety levels in your autistic students?

9. Have you done everything possible to reduce those risks of anxiety for all your autistic students?

Chapter Four

BEHAVIOUR MANAGEMENT AND AUTISM

Steve McNichol and Kersti Duncan

Much training on behaviour management in ITE centres around the Assertive Discipline approach (Canter, 2010) employed by the vast majority of schools. This based on behaviourist principles of rules, rewards and sanctions, which are outlined in the Standard 7 of the Teachers' Standards (DfE, 2011) regarding behaviour management. This can pose problems for teachers in 'managing' the behaviour of autistic pupils.

Firstly, this approach inherently assumes that the behaviour of autistic pupils (and indeed all pupils) is either deliberately 'good' (and therefore deserving of reward) or intentionally 'bad' (and therefore deserving of sanction). However, in the case of autistic pupils, behaviour is more often a form of communication rather than behaviour designed to be challenging. This will be explored further in the next section of this chapter.

Secondly, the use of rewards and sanctions tends to be an ineffective approach for autistic pupils, who often find it difficult to comprehend deferred consequences. The tendency of autistic people to 'live in the moment' means the promise of a future reward or the 'threat' of a future consequence has little or no impact. Given this, it is important that those training new teachers in behaviour management make it clear to trainees that the Assertive Discipline approach is unlikely to be effective when working with autistic pupils and ensure that trainees consider alternative ways of working.

Behaviour is communication

Autism is often characterised by difficulties in communication and interaction. People with autism often find it difficult to understand communication *from* others and also find it difficult to communicate *towards* others. Without knowledge of these comm- unication difficulties, the behaviour of a pupil with autism can be misinterpreted as defiant and a challenge to the teacher's authority. It is important for trainees to understand that often this is not the case and what can appear to be 'challenging behaviour' is usually a result of either a misunderstanding in receptive communication or a difficulty in expressive communication. Knowing that autistic pupils can experience these communication difficulties is essential. When an autistic pupil exhibits behaviour that would usually be considered 'challenging' or 'problematic', it is useful for trainees to consider:

- What might the pupil have missed or misunderstood in terms of communication?

- What might the pupil be trying to communicate through their behaviour?

Often, autistic pupils will have a limited range of communication strategies or an absence of a strategy to enable them to communicate a specific request, emotion or need. This can result in behaviour that can be perceived as 'challenging' but is actually an attempt to communicate.

Hanbury (2007) outlines the four broad areas of need that autistic pupils' communication aims to meet:

- **The need to gain attention.** Autistic pupils may communicate this, for example, through shouting out (which would often be considered low-level disruption).

- **The need for a particular item or activity.** Autistic pupils may communicate this by grabbing items from other children or beginning to undertake an activity at an inappropriate time or place.

- **The need to escape.** Autistic pupils may communicate this through ignoring others (including adults in the classroom!) or running away.

- **The need to relieve sensory 'overload' or meet a sensory need.** Autistic pupils may communicate this through rocking, humming or displaying other behaviour designed to take their focus away from the sensory difficulties they are experiencing.

Task 4.1

Read the case studies below. Discuss the scenarios in pairs or small groups and, in each case, consider what the pupil might be trying to communicate, how you might respond to this communication and how you might approach resolving each situation. Each pair/small group should then feed back on each of these points.

Case study 1

Jack (an autistic child) is in the classroom and you notice that he has sat on his own, away from all other pupils. He has his fingers in his ears. When you approach Jack, he moves away and turns his back on you.

Case study 2

A midday supervisor finds you at lunchtime and explains that Lara (an autistic child) has left the canteen/dining hall without eating any food. Before she left, she shouted at everyone in the room to be quiet then threw her food on the floor. She has now locked herself in a toilet cubicle.

Case study 3

Max (not an autistic child) comes and tells you that Callum (an autistic child) has stolen his coat from the cloakroom to wear outside at breaktime. When Max asked Callum for his coat back, Callum replied that he put it on first and that he will give it back at the end of breaktime.

Case study 4

Your class are working independently when Daniel (an autistic child) starts banging loudly with his fist on his desk. He stamps his feet on the floor and begins to repeatedly stand up and sit down.

Strategies for supporting pupils with autism

Classroom environment

The physical classroom environment can have a significant influence on autistic behaviour (Hanbury, 2007). This is true of the visual appearance of the room, the layout of furniture and the organisation of resources and equipment. Given this, it is reasonable to conclude that changes to the classroom environment can result in changes in the behaviour of those within it. As such, trainees should consider the potential influence of the classroom environment and the impact that making changes to this can have on autistic pupils.

For autistic pupils it is generally accepted that 'low arousal' classroom environments are beneficial to their sense of security. Many autistic pupils find bright, contrasting colours to be overstimulating and therefore it could be beneficial to create a calm visual appearance by using softer 'pastel' colours such as light blues and greens. Many will find posters and wall displays distracting and struggle to filter the input from these, reading and re-reading them. It is also important to create an environment where an autistic child can maintain their personal space and, if possible, to provide an area where they can take themselves away from others. For the following task it is important to provide a variety of examples so that trainees can consider a range of different environments.

Task 4.2

Look at photographs of classrooms and discuss the ways in which these may support autistic pupils, commenting on visual appearance, layout and organisation.

Routines

Many autistic pupils appreciate repetitive routines and procedures. Within the classroom, it is useful to establish and follow these to support the predictability and repetition often needed for autistic pupils to feel safe and comfortable within the classroom environment. Key routines such as entry to the classroom, transitions and specific roles can all be supportive to pupils with autism. For example, going to a set place on entry to the classroom and having a set 'job' at the end of lessons can support autistic pupils within the classroom.

Task 4.3

Make a list of daily routines observed in your classroom/ placement. Discuss with fellow trainees how routines differ between classrooms and how pupils with autism can be supported at these times.

Visual timetables

Visual timetables are portable and adaptable supports which can be presented either horizontally or vertically with laminated picture cards attached to help with communicating the daily activities. Glazzard *et al.* (2015, p.92) argue that use of a visual timetable in the classroom supports a more inclusive philosophy, ensuring that no child is singled out from the rest as all children can understand the daily structure. Research (Goodman and Williams, 2007; Rao and Gagie, 2006; Tissot and Evans, 2003) suggests that some autistic children may think in pictures, finding it easier to process visuals rather than verbal language. As such, the use of visual timetables in the classroom strengthens a child's understanding of what is being communicated to them, enabling them to access the curriculum more effectively. First-hand experiences and Tissot and Evans' (2003) review of literature agree with this, suggesting that teaching methods should place more emphasis on visual approaches rather than auditory instructions to effectively include and promote the progress of autistic pupils. The National Autistic Society (2016) emphasises the importance of making sure that visual supports are appropriate for autistic children, accurately supporting their needs and developmental stage.

Task 4.4

Working in pairs or small groups, create a visual timetable to reflect a regular day at school. Ensure that this shows transitions, lessons (by subject), breaktimes, the location of each activity and the people who will be present. How can you balance the demands of clarity and detail?

Social Stories™

Social Stories™ were designed by Carol Gray in the early 1990s to help autistic individuals to understand social situations and are designed to change specific targeted behaviour. Social Stories™ can be used successfully to support autistic children who find certain situations difficult to comprehend and which can sometimes lead to what others may consider to be inappropriate or challenging behaviour (Timmins, 2016). Social Stories™ are short, visual stories that describe and explain social situations with the aim of providing social information that a child may be misunderstanding or missing. They are written for the specific child and within the specific context of the social interactions they find difficult.

Task 4.5

Read Chapter 8 of Lynn McCann's (2016) book *How to Support Pupils with Autistic Spectrum Condition in Primary School* (this section is relevant to secondary school pupils too).

> How difficult is it to write a Social Story™ for a child who finds a situations difficult (for example, going to assembly, eating in the canteen/dining hall or playing a certain game on the playground)? Do you feel confident writing these stories?

Picture Exchange Communication System (PECS)®

As outlined previously, the behaviour of autistic pupils can often be a consequence of the difficulty they find with communication. One strategy which can be used to support children who experience this barrier is the use of PECS®. This is an alternative communication system which uses icons and pictures to teach the child to initiate conversation by communicating their needs, wants or thoughts through exchanging pictures (McCann, 2016). As some children with ASD may also have delayed language development, the use of PECS® is an appropriate support strategy to support children in their communication skills. Through the use of pictures to communicate meaning, and particularly emotions, pupils are less likely to become frustrated and distressed to the point of exhibiting 'challenging' behaviour.

Image exchange systems work well when the autistic pupil is under stress, as language skills may suffer when the pupil is anxious, angry or overwhelmed. An 'Exit Card' can be presented to the teacher to indicate that the pupil needs time away from the social environment. Similarly, an 'Angry Card' can be used to prevent lashing out and is a way of alerting the teacher to the danger that the autistic pupil is becoming overwhelmed, even though there may be no indication of this.

Task 4.6

What other visual communication cards can you think of? Design cards that would work for you if you suddenly found yourself in an alien environment where your language was not understood.

Summary

Behaviour management continues to be one of the most significant concerns of pre-service teachers during training. Recent emphasis has been given to this area of teacher training through the publication of *Developing Behaviour Management Content for Initial Teacher Training* (Bennett and DfE, 2016). The documentation makes clear that no behaviour management strategy is universally effective (p.9). This is equally true for autistic pupils. Whilst autistic children may share common patterns of behaviour, this is not to say that a strategy that successfully supports one pupil will be successful with another. During training, both when considering behaviour management in general and when exploring strategies to support autistic pupils, trainees should therefore be encouraged to consider various approaches to this aspect of their classroom practice.

References

Canter, L. (2010) *Lee Canter's Assertive Discipline: Positive Behavior Management for Today's Classroom* (4th edn). Bloomington, IN: Solution Tree Press.

Bennett, T. and DfE (Department for Education) (2016) *Developing Behaviour Management Content for Initial Teacher Training (ITT)*. London: DfE.

DfE (Department for Education) (2011) *Teachers' Standards*. London: DfE.

Glazzard, J., Stokoe, J., Hughes, A., Netherwood, A. and Neve, L. (2015) *Teaching and Supporting Children with Special Educational Needs and Disabilities in Primary Schools*. Los Angeles, CA: Sage.

Goodman, G. and Williams, C.M. (2007) Interventions for increasing the academic engagement of students with autism spectrum disorders in inclusive classrooms. *Teaching Exceptional Children 39*, 6, 53–61.

Hanbury, M. (2007) *Positive Behaviour Strategies to Support Children and Young People with Autism.* London: Sage.

McCann, L. (2016) *How to Support Children with Autism Spectrum Condition in Primary School.* Cheshire: Page Bros.

National Autistic Society (2016) Visual supports. Accessed on 09/10/2018 at www.autism.org.uk/about/strategies/visual-supports.aspx

Rao, S.M. and Gagie, B. (2006) Learning through seeing and doing: Visual supports for children with autism. *Teaching Exceptional Children 38*, 6, 26–33.

Timmins, S. (2016) *Successful Social Stories for Young Children.* London: Jessica Kingsley Publishers.

Tissot, C. and Evans, R. (2003) Visual teaching strategies for children with autism. *Early Child Development and Care 173*, 4.

Chapter Five

WHAT WORKS IN AUTISM TRAINING?

Feedback from the Front

Clare Lawrence

When I take feedback from my autism training sessions, the element that is repeatedly reported by the trainees to be most useful is the examples. Telling stories, recalling anecdotes, describing moments, explaining behaviours and relating comments seem to 'bring autism alive' in a way that more factual descriptions of autism do not. This resonates with my own experience. When I started on my own autism journey, by far the best 'education' about autism came from talking to other parents of autistic children. What we feared as odd or unusual in our children could be shared and an understanding emerged that, although each child with autism is entirely unique and the way that autism presents will always be specific to that person, our children were not alone but existed within a 'culture of autism'.

This view of autism as a culture rather than as a string of symptoms is one that very much appeals to me. Yet it is one which is extremely challenging to get across to trainee teachers in the limited time available. Trainee teachers want to know what to do, how to help, what is required to meet the needs of autistic pupils, and the 'culture of autism' approach does not bring easy answers.

Part of the challenge is, I believe, caused by the very training put into place to try to meet it. By providing teacher training 'on autism', we are positioning pupils with autism as being different. I am not denying that difference, or the very real additional challenges that pupils with autism face, or the differentiated teaching they require and deserve, but the positioning of pupils with autism as 'other' remains an issue. Through it we seem to be suggesting that autistic pupils are different and therefore 'not the same' as other pupils, and – by implication – not the same as us, the teachers.

Task 5.1

Identify (hands up, stand up, etc.) if you 'know' someone with autism. What is meant by this is deliberately vague, although if pressed can be qualified as 'being autistic yourself or having a family member or a friend who is autistic'. Do the numbers surprise you?

Discussion point 1

If we each of us carry a village of acquaintances around in our heads – if we each of us 'know' several hundred people – why is it that everyone in the room does not know someone who is autistic? Autism prevalence is believed to be roughly 1 in every 100 of the population. Is the population within the room in some way atypical? Could it be that autism is under-represented in this group? Or could it be that autism is invisible, that people with autism are not disclosing their autism, and in which case, why might that be? If there are more than 100 people present, are there people here who have autism? Are they happy to disclose?

Discussion point 2

Consider the term 'to know' someone in this context. Does the idea of 'knowing' someone carry with it an element of acceptance? Is knowing someone the same as understanding someone? The qualifiers including 'having a friend with autism' – what does that mean given the social challenges inherent in autism? Does the concept of friendship need to be re-evaluated in an autism concept?

The social model of disability (Rieser and Mason, 1990; Tregaskis, 2002) examines the extent to which the 'problems' experienced by individuals seen as disabled are socially constructed rather than intrinsic to the individual. In autism, this model suggests that challenges in, for example, communication may stem as much from the social and educational environment experienced by that individual as from the condition itself (Kossyvaki, Jones and Guldberg, 2016). Given that lack of familiarity with individuals with disabilities may contribute to a person's failure to respect that individual's needs and dignity (Abramson, 2008) and that positive teacher attitudes may be predictors of success in the outcome for pupils with disabilities (Robertson, Chamberlain and Kasari, 2002; Rodriguez, Saldana and Moreno, 2012; Stanovich and Jordan, 1998), it is important for us to consider whether trainee teachers' lack of familiarity with autistic people may contribute towards a negative social model in schools.

The 'mere exposure effect' (Zajonc, 1968) suggests that familiarity with something or someone tends to increase our preference for that item or person and has been used to explore racial prejudice (Zebrowitz, White and Wieneke, 2008), attitudes towards people with intellectual disabilities (Li and Wang, 2013; Rillotta, 2007) and on peer attitudes on first meeting with adults with autism (Sasson and Morrison, 2017). In each case, this research suggested that the participants experienced positive responses from increased exposure to the targeted group. Is a lack of teachers' familiarity with autistic individuals contributing to a lack of acceptance and/or understanding of autistic pupils?

In order to explore whether previous exposure to individuals with autism influenced trainee teachers' initial attitudes towards pupils with autism, I asked 82 third-year undergraduate trainee teachers to self-catagorise themselves as 'knowing' or 'not knowing' someone with autism, and then to give a brief thumbnail sketch how autism might present in a pupil.

Task 5.2

Consider the sample responses given in the table below. Are there qualitative differences in the responses between the two groups? If so, what are they and what might they tell us about the effect of familiarity within this group?

Do not 'know' someone with autism	Do 'know' someone with autism
Social (24%) Pupil may...	**Social (12%)** Pupil may...
• struggle to socialise with peers	• be socially awkward
• find it difficult to make friends	• lack awareness of social rules
• have difficulty understanding the emotions of others	• be trying to impress
• feel 'isolated'	• be keen to talk to strangers but display inappropriate levels of questioning
• be shy and reserved or might prefer their own company	• immerse himself within society to feel part of a group rather than an individual

Emotional (4%)	Emotional (5%)
Pupil may...	Pupil may...
• have 'emotional difficulties'	• have 'high anxiety'
• have difficulty controlling their emotions	• be distressed by confrontations or arguments
• be uncomfortable in new situations	• be someone who 'enjoys own company'
• 'get nervous, stressed, upset easily'	• be initially very shy but also 'creative and sociable'
Communication (9%)	Communication (21%)
Pupil may...	Pupils may...
• 'have communication problems'	• display inappropriate laughter
• 'struggle with communication'	• have delayed speech
• 'have lack of communication'	• speak without thinking
	• enjoy using specific terminology
	• use borrowed language (for example from a screen script) to communicate

Source: Lawrence, 2019

Discussion point

In what ways are the second examples more specific and less generic? Does that very specificity lead to a lack of generalisability, or can it give pointers towards effective differentiation in the classroom?

Differentiation, 'matching teaching to the needs of each learner' (Carolan and Guinn, 2007, p.44), is a particular challenge when teaching autistic pupils because of the heterogeneity of these pupils who are unlike each other, and whose individual needs themselves change according to so many factors. What an individual autistic pupil needs to access your lesson successfully will be different from the needs of another autistic pupil and will change as that child grows up and even day to day, lesson to lesson. This can make the challenge of differentiating your teaching to meet those needs successfully very daunting.

However, perhaps we can learn by taking a look at history. Autistic people are statistically 'different' in that they make up a relatively small percentage of the population. The predominant neurotype is just that: predominant. A similar neurological subtype exists in those who favour the use of their left hand over their right. In less enlightened times, those who were left-handed have been condemned as 'sinister', 'gauche' and 'cack-handed'. They were encouraged, even forced, to use their right hands and to conform to the predominant norm. Is there something we can learn from the treatment in education of this previously vilified section of the population?

We no longer view left-handedness as a disability. It is no longer used as a descriptor for an individual (other than in sport, it is unusual to hear someone described as 'a left-hander'), and we no longer seek to correct left-handedness, to bring these people in line with the predominant neurotype. To this extent, there is much that could be learned in the way we view autistic pupils.

On the other hand, do we really differentiate for these pupils as much as we should in schools? Has acceptance brought with it a complacency, and an unwillingness to – or a lack of perception of the need to – adapt?

Task 5.3

In groups, list all of the ways that we should/could be differentiating to better meet the needs of left-handed pupils. Include seating plans (to accommodate handwriting position), sports, musical instruments, demonstration by right-handed teachers, science apparatus…

Discussion point

How could we accommodate left-handers' needs more effectively in the classroom? Is there a case for employing a left-handed teaching assistant if the teacher is right-handed? What if the teacher is left-handed?

Continue this discussion, this time for pupils who are autistic. Are there parallels? Is there anything we can learn from left-handedness that we could adapt to similarly meet the needs of autistic learners?

Conclusions

In this chapter, we have considered something of our positioning of autistic pupils as 'other'. We have considered what this 'otherness' suggests about our attitudes and our acceptance, and have considered how greater visibility, acknowledgement, understanding and familiarity with autistic people might improve teachers' understanding of the needs of autistic pupils in their classes.

However, we have also considered the dangers of too great an acceptance. If the autistic population in our schools is not recognised as 'different', there is a danger that their needs will not be differentiated for in our lessons. Understanding should bring greater accommodation of children's individual needs, not less.

To finish:

Task 5.4

Feedback from my training sessions on autism suggests that one of the most useful elements in autism understanding is the sharing of stories and anecdotes. In your groups, those of you who do 'know' people with autism take some time to describe what is interesting, unusual or intriguing about these people. Some of your stories may well be funny, and that is OK too. As long as it is used affectionately – and you are laughing with and not at – humour can be a great way to break down barriers and to bring what is perceived as 'other' into our shared 'norm'. Take some time to enjoy autism's differentness; I believe that it is truly fascinating.

References

Abramson, B. (2008) *Article 2: The Right of Non-discrimiation.* Boston, MA: Martinus Nijhoss Publishers.

Carolan, J. and Guinn, A. (2007) Differentiation: Lessons from master teachers. *Educational Leadership 64,* 5, 44–47.

Kossyvaki, L., Jones, G. and Guldberg, K. (2012) The effect of adult interactive style on the spontaneous communication of young children with autism at school. *British Journal of Special Education 39,* 4, 173–184.

Lawrence, C. (2019) The effect of familiarisation with autistic individuals on trainee teachers' attitudes. *Teacher Education Advancement Network Journal 11,* 1, 37–45.

Li, C. and Wang, C.K.J. (2013) Effect of exposure to Special Olympic Games on attitudes of volunteers towards inclusion of people with intellectual disabilities. *Journal of Applied Research in Intellectual Disabilities 26,* 6, 515–521.

Rieser, R. and Mason, M. (1990) *Disability Equality in the Classroom: A Human Rights Issue.* London: Disability Equality in Education.

Rillotta, F.A. (2007) Effects of an awareness program on attitudes of students without an intellectual disability towards persons with an intellectual disability. *Journal of Intellectual and Developmental Disability 32,* 1, 19–27.

Robertson, K., Chamberlain, B. and Kasari, C. (2003) General education teachers' relationships with included students with autism. *Journal of Autism and Developmental Disorders 33,* 2, 123–130.

Rodriguez, I.R., Saldana, D. and Moreno, F.J. (2012) Support, inclusion and special education teachers' attitudes towards the education of students with autism spectrum disorders. *Autism Research and Treatment.* Accessed on 09/10/2018 at www.hindawi.com/journals/aurt/2012/259468

Sasson, N.J and Morrison, K.E. (2017) First impressions of adults with autism improve with diagnostic disclosure and increased autism knowledge of peers. *Autism*. doi: 10.1177/1362361317729526

Stanovich, P.J. and Jordan, A. (1998) Canadian teachers' and principals' beliefs about inclusive education as predictors of effective teaching in heterogeneous classrooms. *The Elementary School Journal 98*, 3, 221–238.

Tregaskis, C. (2002) Social model theory, the story so far... *Disability & Society 17*, 4, 457–470.

Zajonc, R.B. (1968) Attitudinal effects of mere exposure. *Journal of Personality and Social Psychology 9, 2, Pt.2*, 1–27.

Zebrowitz, L.A., White, B. and Wieneke, K. (2008) Mere exposure and racial prejudice: Exposure to other-race faces increases liking for strangers of that race. *Social Cognition 26*, 3, 259–275.

Chapter Six

AUTISM AND MATHS

The Strengths, Challenges and Dangers of Making Assumptions

Shaun Thompson

There is increased pressure on schools to ensure children meet expected levels of attainment in maths. Whilst significant research has been previously carried out to determine the overall mathematical problem-solving ability of autistic pupils, and in particular the effectiveness of short-term interventions, according to Keen, Webster and Ridley, 2015, there remains a distinct lack of research to bridge the gap between understanding the nature of academic achievement for individuals with autism and working with educators to create practices that support autistic individuals to achieve academic success (Keen *et al.*, 2015).

Furthermore, within the new national curriculum for England there is an increased emphasis on problem solving in mathematics. Within the UK there is a significant influence on the school curriculum that is driven by the results of international comparative assessments such as the Programme for International Student Assessment (PISA).

Influences from those countries who demonstrate higher levels of performance than the UK, particularly in mathematics – for example many South East Asian countries such as Singapore and China – frequently impact upon the classroom practice and curriculum development of schools in England. As educators, we need to make certain that we can bridge the gap between research and practice to ensure that the learning differences sometimes demonstrated by those autistic pupils within our classes are understood, met and utilised.

Previous research identified a need for further research into potential factors that support mathematical word problem-solving ability for autistic students as a prerequisite for supporting these pupils in the general mathematics curriculum (Bae, Chiang and Hickson, 2015). They go on to state that little is still known about research within the context of any specific models or theoretical frameworks for this group of individuals.

So, what does the current research say? According to the research, it is suggested that between 6 and 22 per cent of autistic children and adolescents are reported to struggle with number and calculation, to an extent where their mathematical difficulties are incommensurate with their intellectual functioning (Aagten-Murphy *et al.*, 2015) yet there are remarkably few research studies addressing this issue. This study, therefore, sought to examine autistic children's number estimation skills and whether variation in these skills can explain at least in part strengths and weaknesses in children's mathematical achievement. Thirty-two cognitively able children with autism (range = 8–13 years).

When it comes to solving mathematical word problems, there is a requirement for the integration of several cognitive processes and it is suggested that a focus on the teaching of mathematical vocabulary may improve students' mathematical performance (Fletcher and Santoli, 2003). Thus, an autistic individual's ability with mathematical vocabulary may be synonymous with their ability in problem solving.

Subsequent research has also identified a need for teachers to focus on other skills, such as reading comprehension, computation and an understanding of the individual's everyday mathematical knowledge, in order to support the development of problem-solving abilities amongst autistic individuals (Bae *et al.*, 2015; Boonen *et al.*, 2013; Siegel, 2009; Wei *et al.*, 2015).

In terms of important pedagogical approaches within the classroom, and considerations to be made when designing and implementing interventions, it is suggested that providing autistic individuals with choices, having an awareness of pupils' interests and incorporating these into teaching, and adapting the curriculum to meet individual needs may all be pertinent to their mathematical success (Banda *et al.*, 2007).

Mathematical problem solving has also been identified as an area where autistic individuals particularly appeared to achieve disproportionately to that of their peers (Keen *et al.*, 2015; Troyb *et al.*, 2014).

So, as practitioners, thus far, the key factors emerging from the literature to support mathematical problem solving within the autistic population should give some consideration to the factors represented in Figure 6.1, which consolidates the findings from the literature.

In terms of everyday mathematical knowledge, it is suggested that non-autistic individuals have a higher level than those with autism (Bae *et al.*, 2015). Also, it has been suggested that non-autistic pupils are able to distinguish between their 'everyday' mathematical knowledge and the esoteric knowledge – or that which is required to be drawn upon when answering problem-solving questions in mathematics.

Figure 6.1 Mathematical reasoning v communication

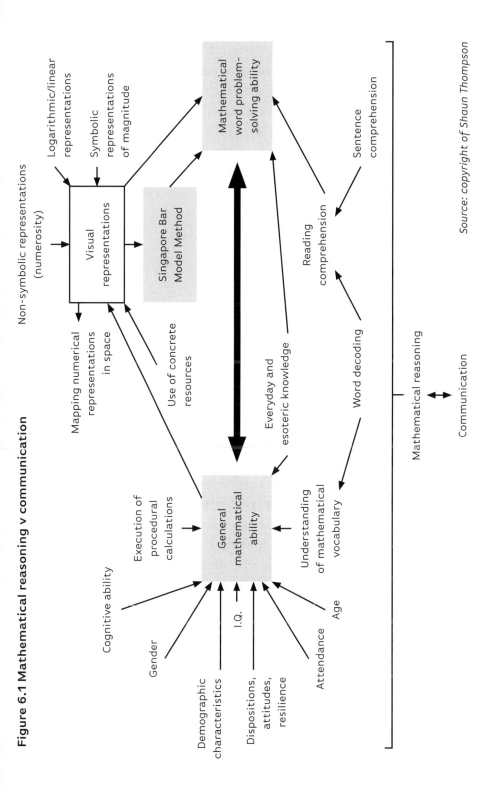

Source: copyright of Shaun Thompson

According to Bae *et al.*, 2015 everyday mathematical knowledge refers to the mathematical concepts that are learned in everyday experiences and contexts, and it is often regarded as 'mathematical background knowledge' or 'real-world knowledge'. In order to successfully solve a word problem, a student needs to link the problem to a real-world situation and select appropriate mathematical operations and skills. The weakness in everyday mathematical knowledge in autistic children may be due to their limited community experiences and restricted and repetitive patterns of behaviour, interests or activities. Let's look at an example of where this may become problematic.

Task 6.1

What's the answer?

James wants to put up some shelves, each two metres in length. He has four pieces of wood, each with a length of 2.5 metres. How many shelves can he make?

Most people would answer five – after all, in a test situation that is what would be expected. However, draw on your experiential knowledge. Are you really going to make a shelf out of four separate pieces of wood? Probably not, in which case you are only going to make four shelves. Yet there's that fine line in education, which requires us to be able to distinguish between what the correct answer would be in a mathematics lesson or a test and what the answer would be in real life – depending upon our ability to distinguish between these two types of knowledge.

So, for the autistic pupil who is insistent on arguing the answer to be four, this presents us with some potential difficulties as educators. As there is a focus on the use of mathematics in real-life contexts, as educators, we need to think very carefully about how 'realistic' the real-life contexts are in which we frame our mathematics.

Think about the 'reality' of these 'real-life' questions:

I had 51 lizards. Mum gave me 16 more. How many lizards have I got now?

There were 34 lions at the zoo. 19 more came from another zoo. How many lions were there altogether?

Often, without even realising it, the mathematical questions we ask children are based on assumptions – assumptions that we wouldn't question the fact that a zoo would really have 53 lions and that it would be realistic to have 77 lizards, and so on.

Remember, one size does not fit all; don't fall into the trap of stereotypes.

Task 6.2

Write down the first things that come to mind when you think about supporting autistic pupils within the classroom (in mathematics and the wider curriculum).

No doubt on your list are things like:

- visual timetables

- choices

- processing time

- communication books

- vocabulary development

- Social Stories™

- transition passports

- iPad apps.

Whilst some of these strategies and approaches may well be beneficial to some autistic pupils, as educators it is important that we do not make assumptions based on our stereotypes. Some of you may well be thinking, 'but autistic people are really good at maths' – this may be true for some children, but is it the case for all?

The essential component to high-quality teaching and learning for autistic pupils in the classroom relies on a fundamental principle:

> Know the pupil as an individual – what are their strengths and areas of difficulty? How do they learn most effectively? What are their barriers to learning?

Only through considering the autistic pupil(s) within your mathematics lesson as individuals can you really begin to support them and create a truly inclusive mathematics classroom.

Let'ss consider an example. Louis is very able when it comes to manipulating numbers and mental calculations. He can very quickly recall multiplication facts and identify patterns in number sequences. He is able to add two 3-digit numbers mentally with ease most of the time, and this is his default method of choice for such calculations.

Now imagine your mathematics lesson today is focusing on the use and application of the grid method for multiplication. Despite clearly modelling this, Louis reverts back to using mental calculation strategies and always gets the correct answer. You can begin to see levels of frustration rising. Why might this be? He has got the correct answer, however he is not using the grid method – the purpose of the lesson.

Consider this from Louis' perspective:

- Why do I need to use the grid method when I already know how to get the answer?

- What's the point of using the grid method when I can get the same answer using my own method (mental calculation)?

From Louis' perspective, the task is meaningless – there is no point in doing this when he can already get the answer using mental calculation. This scenario occurred in a case study I carried out last year and the teacher explained what was going on:

- Louis was in his comfort zone when using his mental calculation strategies, as this was a particular area of mathematics which was his strength.

- Through risk of failure to get the correct answer using the grid method, he was not comfortable using this approach with which he was unfamiliar, when he was sure he could get the right answer using his own approach.

Consequently, the teacher found the need to consider modelling specific examples where he could 'prove' to Louis that the grid method was an easier and more efficient method. For example, he was aware that the increase on Louis' cognitive load through using a calculation where all of the numbers would cross the hundreds, tens and ones boundary would make it more difficult for Louis to mentally calculate the solution:

e.g. $477 + 788 =$

Only through 'proving' to Louis that the grid method may be more efficient for this calculation, did Louis begin to utilise this approach.

So, as teachers, what does this suggest?

- The need to understand Louis as an individual and be aware of his strengths and barriers to learning (cognitive load in this case).

- The need to consider very carefully the 'purpose' of the mathematics we are using.

- The need to consider very carefully the choice of calculations used to model the method and to ask Louis to solve.

In thise example, when the teacher was attempting to demonstrate a more efficient method of addition to Louis, the teacher commented that he insisted on reverting back to less efficient methods with which he was more familiar. It wasn't until Louis made an error with his method, due to the use of larger numbers being modelled by the teacher, that he began to utilise the more efficient method.

The teacher also talked about the importance of contextualising the learning for this individual and drawing on his experiential knowledge, enabling him to link mathematical processes to real-life situations or context he was familiar with.

One of the key strategies believed to be significant by the teacher in this study was that of disproving or highlighting the inefficiencies in the pupil's methods in which he was already secure. This was often backed up with modelling and sometimes the use of concrete or visual approaches thus making clear representation to the pupil as to context or situations that his method may not be successful.

So far, we have looked at some inclusive practices that may support autistic individuals with mathematical problem solving. However, at this point it is also worth considering how our own practice in the classroom may potentially lead to exclusion for these pupils.

For example, by not incorporating some of the practices already discussed, we may indeed be unintentionally excluding some of these individuals. This may be through imposing our own preferred methods on to the pupils, through a lack of awareness of the individual's experiential learning needs or failing to provide the opportunity for the pupils to make choices. It is also quite frequently through the provision of adult support, which whilst it may be seen as inclusive practice, may in fact prevent some pupils from maximising their potential through the application of their own preferred methods.

Task 6.3

Look back at Chapter One, 'Understanding Autism', and consider the cognitive theories which underpin autism

— theory of mind, weak central coherence and executive functioning. How might some of these difficulties manifest themselves in the mathematics classroom? In which particular aspects of mathematics might we begin to see difficulties arising? What strategies, as a teacher, might you consider in order to support these particular difficulties in mathematics?

So, to conclude, ensuring that mathematics in mainstream schools is inclusive for those autistic pupils within our classes doesn't necessarily require significant changes in our practice. More, it is a case of recognising those differences and drawing on the findings from current research to ensure that simple approaches, such as providing choices, contextualising learning, being aware of the importance of reading comprehension and mathematical vocabulary and the impact these factors may have on allowing those autistic individuals to thrive within our classrooms.

References

Aagten-Murphy, D., Attucci, C., Daniel, N., Klaric, E., Burr, D.C. and Pellicano, E. (2015) Numerical estimation in children with autism. *Autism Research 8*, 6, 668–681.

Bae, Y.S., Chiang, H.-M. and Hickson, L. (2015) Mathematical word problem solving ability of children with autism pectrum disorder and their typically developing peers. *Journal of Autism and Developmental Disorders 45*, 7, 2200–8. Accessed on 09/10/2018 at https://doi.org/10.1007/s10803-015-2387-8

Banda, D.R., McAfee, J.K., Lee, D.L., Kubina, R.M., James, R.B. and Mcafee, K. (2007) Math preference and mastery relationship in middle school students with autism spectrum disorders. *Journal of Behavioral Education 16*, 3, 207–223.

Boonen, A.J.H., van der Schoot, M., van Wesel, F., de Vries, M.H. and Jolles, J. (2013) What underlies successful word problem solving? A path analysis in sixth grade students. *Contemporary Educational Psychology 38*, 3, 271–279. Accessed on 09/10/2018 at https://doi.org/10.1016/j.cedpsych.2013.05.001

Fletcher, M. and Santoli, S. (2003) Reading to learn concepts in mathematics: An action research project. *ERIC*. Accessed on 23/10/2018 at https://files.eric.ed.gov/fulltext/ED482001.pdf

Keen, D., Webster, A. and Ridley, G. (2015) How well are children with autism spectrum disorder doing academically at school? An overview of the literature. *Autism 20*, 3, 276–294.

Siegel, B. (2009) Treatment Options for Autistic Spectrum Disorders: An Overview. Accessed on 09/10/2018 at www.ucsfcme.com/2008/MOC08001/SiegelTreatmentOptionsForAutismSpectrumDisorders.pdf

Troyb, E., Orinstein, A., Tyson, K., Helt, M. *et al.* (2014) Academic abilities in children and adolescents with a history of autism spectrum disorders who have achieved optimal outcomes. *Autism 18*, 3, 233–243. Accessed on 09/10/2018 at https://doi.org/10.1177/1362361312473519

Wei, X., Christiano, E.R., Yu, J.W., Wagner, M. and Spiker, D. (2015) Reading and math achievement profiles and longitudinal growth trajectories of children with an autism spectrum disorder. *Autism 19*, 2, 200–210.

Chapter Seven

THE *DREADED* PHYSICAL EDUCATION LESSONS

Managing the Challenges that PE and PESS Lessons Can Raise for Children with Autism

Helen Thornalley

Aims of the chapter

Educationalists state that there is an emergent need to work more productively with autistic learners, not just because of their academic rights or because of the therapeutic advantages that exercise gives them, but because of the reality that schools are finding they have more identified autistic children trying to access learning within in their classroom (Boucher, 2017). This chapter aims to:

- understand why physical education and school sports (PESS) are essential for pupils with autism

- visualise how events found in PESS sessions impact on the success of these learners

- use practical examples and vignettes to unpick some of the realities for the learner, support teacher and teacher.

The focus

The focus for this chapter has been positioned through the experiences and observations of training and working with physical education (PE) teachers at secondary and primary levels and conducting scholarly and research projects within a range of school provision: tennis (Thornalley, 2017), dance (Thornalley, 2015–2018), postgraduate teaching experiences (Thornalley, 2012) and vulnerable learners in school (Howe and Thornalley, 2019). Attention in this chapter focuses on lesson planning and how time, space and sensory experiences all affect pupils with autism, and how all of these influences have positive and negative implications for their success (Boucher, 2017).

The essential requirement for obtaining the most from this chapter is that you have an awareness of the need to adapt pedagogy to suit different types of learners. You should draw on past experiences and experientially develop these instances into tangible pedagogic processes for the future. This process then will become a continuous cycle of progress planning: action, reflection and modification (Ball, 2013; Sandt, 2013; Smith, Donlan and Smith, 2012).

The challenge

Autistic children are a group for whom moderate to vigorous physical activity (MVPA) targets are continually missed and who are frequently found to have motor skills challenges and sensory extremes of under- and over-development. Each of these may add to the barriers that these learners face when developing physical literacy (Yianni-Coudurier *et al.,* 2008). The International Physical Literacy Association (IPLA) (2017) describes physical literacy as: 'the motivation, confidence, physical competence, knowledge and understanding to value and take responsibility for engagement in physical activities for life'.

The reality for many teachers is that there is an observable reduction in physical activity with children with autism, with these pupils consistently underachieving in age-related activities. Physical education and school sports teachers therefore need to understand the challenges that these pupils have prior to, during and after PE lessons (Law *et al.,* 2006; Pan, Tsai and Hsieh, 2011; Rosser-Sandt and Grey 2005). The challenge with these pupils is both that they may enjoy sedentary behaviours because these can often occur in insolation, but that they also find PE activities more challenging than their peers because of their biological physical literacy and social sensory traits.

The challenges for teachers of autistic pupils in PESS are:

- to help develop pupils' anatomical embodiment (an awareness of movement through the body) (IPLA, 2017; Whitehead, 2010)

- to allow them to understand the relevancy of the subject in their life and well-being (Meckbach *et al.,* 2014)

- to consider how to engage with PESS in different way (Tinning *et al.,* 1993)

- to enable pupils in turn to *not* dread physical activities (PA).

These four objectives for PESS teachers are, in many ways, no different to the challenge they have with all learners. Many pupils dislike PESS because they prefer to be sedentary (Bailey *et al.,* 2009; Kirk, 2011) and suggestions from the beginning of the 1990s indicated that Britain then, and now, continues to be the leading nation in heart disease (BHF, 2017). Very few children exercise outside of school as cultural changes have encouraged leisure time to be spent indoors (Almond, 1997; Little, 2015). 'Activity levels remain low and are continuing to fall' (Thornalley, 2017, p.4) but, as Talbot suggests as chief executive of the Association for Physical Education (AfPE), PESS 'involves both "learning to move" and "moving to learn" through a range of performing environments within and after school, thus the challenge remains consistent for all' (2001, p.31).

For learning and teaching to be successful:

- it must be guided from a teacher's own past experiences and the power of the pedagogic stories that they have or can draw from

- physical literacy must underpin everything that is central to teaching learners in PESS

- teachers' past experiences must be used to create knowledge that is continually adapted for different learners.

Task 7.1

What elements may make your autistic learners vulnerable and disadvantaged in PESS? What adaptations do you currently plan to meet the needs of your autistic learners?

A brief overview of current practice

Literature supporting educational strategies used with autistic pupils' learning in PA is limited when it comes to practical application. This current reality may be because there has been no statutory obligation for teachers to be trained specifically in teaching children with autism and within initial teacher training (ITT) provision the work with autistic learners often falls under the banner of special educational needs (SEN). In addition to this, PESS specialists frequently focus on physical disabilities within their subject training and cater for these learners through modifying equipment so they may participate. Supplementary to this reality on teacher training requirements, it is known that those who move into training to teach and those that teach their trainees all hold a set of values on what the subject should look like and how it should be experienced, all of which stems from their own experiences and lies very much in the competence-based model for the physically able learner (Capel *et al.*, 2016; Darling-Hammond, 2000; Shulman, 1987). This could be why many autistic children dread PE lessons because there is limited understanding in PE staff about how to plan for their needs (Davies, 2017; Weber, 2017).

However, there are good examples of how support materials can link pedagogy and teacher planning together and there are teachers in mainstream and special schools who champion the skills needed for teaching pupils with autism. The National Autistic Society, and in particular the work by Weber (2017), is one such champion. Within this source a young rugby player is used as a case study in the form of a vignette to highlight that autistic individuals can succeed in (team) sport and the life skills he has learnt through playing sport. This working document is filled with work sheets and probing questions that individuals can use with learners, teachers and support staff but more importantly this shows there is not an inevitable ceiling for pupils with autism in the subject of PESS.

Government expectations: Physical Education National Curriculum (PENC)

The PENC (DfE, 2014) runs across all four Key Stages and requires the subject to be taught by specialist and non-specialist teachers depending on the school. What is significant about PE is that it remains the only subject during this journey that does not have to be formally examined at any point. Therefore, the subject's design is often undertaken solely through the mastery of skilled teachers who interpret and then translate the PENC through their vision.

The PENC asks teachers and support staff to create learning events that allow pupils to be:

- physically active for sustained periods of time

- competitive with themselves and others

- inspired to lead healthier lives.

Each of these is generic, non-specific and potentially difficult to measure.

The Department for Education does not give specific guidance for PE teachers within the National Curriculum documents on how to solve the questions of what to teach and how (Key Stages 1 to 4). At no point in the policies does it state that learners must play games such as football, that they must be able to catch, throw or roll, or that swimming as an essential life skill must competently be mastered. What the curriculum does offer is a broad landscape to which teachers can create Schemes of Work (SoW) that challenge learners through a range of physical activities.

Therefore, if the curriculum and its content have a relatively open platform, why is it that children with autism often feel that PESS is not for them when the content of what is being taught can undoubtedly be changed?

Government expectations: Teachers' Standards

In addition, teacher quality is practically translated through the Department for Education's statutory Teachers' Standards (TS) (DfE, 2013). These are seen as the backbone to all trainee teachers' guidance and continue throughout a teacher's career.

Teachers' Standards One to Five offer a generic but transferable requirement to:

- TS1: inspire and motivate pupils

- TS2: ensure pupils make progress

- TS3: teach through subject and curriculum knowledge

- TS4: plan and teach structured lessons

- TS5: adapt teaching to respond to the strengths and need of all pupils.

It is in TS4 and TS5 that the professional expectations, qualities and endeavours of teaching staff underpin each of the previous standards.

School experience

The cultural environment of each school also plays a significant role in the subject's provision. If the school does not have a swimming pool there is an increased chance that swimming will not be covered. If the subject teacher's own specialism is rugby then rugby is likely to be on the curriculum. If the headteacher strives for their school to be competitively successful then structures to support this will be found in and outside school competitions and if the school does not deploy support staff into PESS sessions because of funding priorities, then children with learning disabilities may be left to cope with the challenges of the lesson on their own.

What does this mean for children with autism? They may be vying for the attention of the class teacher along with possibly 30 other pupils in activities in which they may not feel safe or which they may not enjoy. PESS then becomes that dreaded lesson as pupils struggle with what is being demanded of them. They may not enjoy the physical activity selected; they may have no desire to exercise away from the lesson and find a sedentary lifestyle much more appealing (BHF, 2017; WHO, 2013).

Consequently, it is no surprise that if the teacher is not well skilled in adapting learning episodes for children with autism or if they feel that these pupils are not a priority, autistic pupils will be lost within the process of teaching that could have been adapted (Qi and Ha, 2012). These professional reflections signify the feeling that teaching will not be complying with TS4 and TS5 and that pupils with autism are not be being treated differently in order that they can become equal.

Planning

When planning lessons, the following elements should be considered:

- There is a danger that many teachers plan to the middle band of learners and quantify the processes of the lesson on what the majority of the class can do in the allotted time frames.

- There is a danger that teaching and learning is favourable for extrovert learners.

Therefore, when planning for autistic learners, teachers must further consider:

- how these individual learners cope with the different domains of the lesson – changing rooms, equipment management, transfer to teaching areas, working in different spaces with different conditions (weather related)

- their understanding of the anatomical capability of the autistic pupil and their sensory development

- if the autistic learners in the class can obtain the learning objectives through reciprocal learning (group tasks) (Mosston and Ashworth, 2008).

Task 7.2

Using the following two case studies, think through the learning needs and experience these learners may have in PESS sessions.

Case study 1: Kit is King for Robert

Robert is autistic and a very quiet boy who is anatomically smaller than many of his classmates. He is very well presented at school and has a real level of pride when it comes to his school uniform and PE kit.

Robert is very organised and has all of his personal items labelled and packed in particular ways. He enjoys organising his kit for the different activities and particularly enjoys wearing his rugby jersey but does not like his athletics vest or his kit getting dirty.

Rugby is Robert's favoured activity. He really enjoys running freely with the ball but he struggles with contact activities in tackling and forming mini scrums. During learning conversations in lessons, he contributes very little and seems to only speak to one other individual in the group.

Discussion points

1. Is there a particular learning strategy that you would use to get Robert to love his rugby but also other activities he needs to cover on the curriculum?

2. What additional modifications would you have in place for Robert when playing games and practising aspects of play?

3. Robert is confident when performing in isolation but has a tendency to not stay focused for the duration of the lesson. How would you address this?

4. Do you think there would be a concern regarding Robert's love of his kit?

Case study 2: Bridget needs quiet

Bridget is an individual who thrives in the arenas of physical education although her levels of communication and emotional state can be affected if she loses in activities or disagrees with peers' thoughts. Bridget enjoys social company and has a small, close network of friends. However, few of these friends are in her PE class.

Bridget changes for PE lessons quickly and is always keen to build the learning environment through equipment organisation. However, for Bridget noise levels and ensuring that she absorbs instructions are difficult, and these areas can lead to increased anxiety. Bridget has a learning assistant in the room but feels that she does not need this support as she loves the subject.

Bridget is confident when playing netball and volleyball and enjoys telling others what to do on the court. However, she is reluctant to change positions or be substituted during these games.

Discussion points

1. Which lesson elements would need to be modified for Bridget and why?

2. What should the role of the learning assistant be with regard to supporting Bridget?

3. What additional modifications would you need to have in place when playing games that involve Bridget?

Learning cues and lesson planning for autistic pupils

During the lesson when looking at movement replication skills and responding to performance cues (which all PA requires), two significant factors may affect these implementation outcomes for autistic learners. These are:

- the anatomical function (physical movement)

- the application process (when to perform).

These combine with the reality that pupils with autism may have reduced muscle tone, reduced coordination skills, and gross and fine muscle difficulties, all of which significantly influence activities of reaction and recall. The ability to produce sustained moments of exercise means that autistic pupils may have a tendency to fatigue and to giving up more easily (Chroinin, Fletcher and O'Sullivan, 2017). Pupils with autism may dislike flying balls or fast-moving pieces of equipment plus they may have spatial awareness challenges that counter the requirements of game play and safety. Sensory receptors associated with hearing, smell, balance and control can also be creating difficulties for pupils to perform in spaces and within allotted time frames. PESS requires so many senses to function, not only in a particular range but often at the same time, and it is this that makes PESS uniquely different to any other subject in school.

The development of ideas on identifying where and how cues for learning in PESS can be made successful for all is through the deconstruction of sensory attentions (Leekam *et al.*, 2007) and in particular the taxonomy created by Menear and Smith (2011). The understanding of sensory inputs gives additional depth of understanding of how learners learn and how senses influence successes. Several scholars such at Leekam *et al.* (2007) and Lee and Haegele (2016) support these notions and suggest that as with all interpretations of the world and the challenges offered, responses are built around recognising cues so that we behave in appropriate ways.

Interpretation of the five challenge categories (Menear and Smith 2011)

Menear and Smith define the sensory inputs into five challenging categories: visual, auditory, tactile, proprioceptive and vestibular.

They advocate that planning for this type of learning should take into account each of these categories.

Task 7.3

Using the examples of the visual challenges below, deconstruct the remaining senses into organisation and pedagogic planning that might support an autistic pupil.

Visual challenge: interventions/modifications

Equipment is colour coded so that pupils can recognise their own specific piece of equipment. There are clear boundaries as to the areas the pupil can move within and routines are established that can be replicated, such as walking particular ways to the performance area 'down the green corridor, through the red doors'.

Visual pedagogic ideas

Teach movement in skills development and sequences of learning processes through visual demonstrations routines.

Visual learning support

Pupils have learning buddies who can assist them in the skill development where they are the (visual) performance model for them. Learners work within similar ability groups so that performance is relatively close to their own success outcome and thus built on goal similarity.

Other challenges: auditory, tactile, proprioceptive, vestibular. Reflect on activity, location, working with, equipment, noises and danger.

Lesson time, planning time

When is learning taking place in the PESS lesson?

In many classroom-based learning environments the transition from arriving at the lesson and the activation of the first learning activity is quite quick but for many teachers of PESS a minimum of 10 minutes can be lost from the start: there is the transfer to wherever teaching space has been allocated and this is the same at the end of the lesson. Thus, logistical organisation of self, equipment and learners working with others must be brought into planning and considered in three lesson planning time zones:

- changing time (CT)

- equipment time (ET)

- content learning time (CLT).

Task 7.4

Reflect on the different time spaces that an autistic pupil has to navigate through in order to access learning in a PE/sport lesson. What are the inherent challenges and dangers of each space and time zone? How could you support autistic pupils to better negotiate each of CT, ET and CLT?

You will have to consider the following fixed elements in this reflection: distance from previous lesson, space outside the changing facilities for lining up, space inside the changing facility, distance from the changing room to the learning space, where the equipment cupboards are, the equipment needed to play the activity.

Use the strengths, weaknesses, opportunities, threats (SWOT) analysis on the 'Time and location: changing rooms' handout (see Table 7.1) to support consideration of the challenges for autistic pupils.

Table 7.1 Time and location: changing rooms

Strengths	Weaknesses
• The process of changing out of uniform into kit is a routine: it is at the start and end of every lesson and is very prescribed, e.g. time length and what clothes to wear.	• The correct kit for the lesson has to be brought to school.
	• If lesson activity (content) is changed it may require different kit that the pupil does not have.
• The changing process can be practised away from the changing room.	• PESS kit can have a range of different textures that some pupils do not like.
• If unsure of what is required during changing time pupils can copy each other to complete the task.	• If part of the uniform is forgotten the wearing of other parts may be less desirable, e.g. forgotten socks, or may create a higher risk of incident, e.g. no studs in boots, no shin pads, no rugby shirt, no gum shield.
• Pupils begin to have pride in wearing kit. This can be very motivational to learners who see the need for kit to be worn because that is what we exercise in.	• Changing has to take place in a communal space.

Opportunities	Threat
• The pupil can demonstrate the ability to change from uniform to kit and vice versa with speed and ease.	• The time given to pupils to change is too short.
• The pupil can demonstrate the ability to complete the changing task in a fluid space.	• The changing room has no seating plan and there is often an inconsistency of where changing takes place.
• Organisation of correct kit and organisation of clothes that can be taken off can be practised and refined.	• The closeness to others in the changing area is distracting.
	• The potential loss of uniform once taken off is unnerving.
	• The smell of the changing rooms is threatening.
	• The pupil may fear that kit will become dirty due to physical activity.
	• Exposing the body to others is unmarshaled.

Potential adjustment

The following is a list of potential 'reasonable adjustments' that could be made to support an autistic pupil through the 'changing time' element of a PESS lesson:

1. Encourage/enable the learner to arrive early (for example, during breaktimes).

2. Grant the pupil direct access into the changing space rather than having to line up outside.

3. Allocate places in the changing room to reduce stress of decision making (and the potential for bullying).

4. Practise changing into kit (at home and in school).

5. Provide a physical exercise purpose (warm up or gathering equipment) to the distance time from the changing room to the learning space.

6. Allocate autistic individuals roles to help lead and support during transition to learning space.

Task 7.5

What further reasonable adjustments can you suggest to support autistic learners through the other elements of the lesson (ET, CLT)?

Conclusion

The aim of the chapter has been to begin a strategic conversation that supports professionals in all stages of their career. The interrogation of the knowledge that is currently used about the autistic child's humanistic and behavioural strength alongside policy expectations for teacher trainer and trainee teacher is an essential one. If we consider all of the points presented in this chapter, the debate needs to further continue about why children with autism may be receiving PESS that is inconsistently working for them and, on many occasions, may be dreaded by them.

The demands that are being made on teachers continue to grow as we move through the 21st century (Lytle *et al.*, 2003). Movements in examination subjects, diversity of learners in classrooms and the pastoral care that is being asked of teachers requires that professionals be masters of many aspects of modern education. Policy makers and academics alike agree that the profession has countless demands and that contemporary teachers are tasked with rotating roles that they must be highly qualified in and have a 'comprehensive content knowledge on teaching children' (Columna *et al.*, 2014, p.485).

However, regardless of these demands, the needs of autistic learners in PESS must not be overlooked. PESS teachers need to consider, consciously, the needs of their autistic learners, and how reducing these learners' anxieties may make them more able to learn. Teachers must ensure that they do not ignore concerns because of very real difficulties in communicating with families and the learner. They need to instigate different feedback and reflective provision so that a cycle of progressive planning informs their practice (Bucek, 2018; Howe and Thornalley, 2019). Many autistic learners may not have intrinsic motivation, interest, curiosity and enjoyment in PESS (Brewster and Fager, 2000), but by looking at what we offer them and considering PESS lessons through their eyes, we may find ways to better support these children to develop towards more active, more confident and healthier lives.

References

Almond, L. (1997) *Physical Education in Schools* (2nd edn). London: Kogan Page Limited.

Bailey, R., Armour, K., Kirk, D., Jess, M. *et al.* (2009) The educational benefits claimed for physical education and school sport: An academic review. *Research Papers in Education 24*, 1, 1–27.

Ball, S.J. (2013) *Education, Justice and Democracy: The Struggle over Ignorance and Opportunity.* London: Centre for Labour and Social Studies.

Boucher, J. (2017) *Autism Spectrum Disorder: Characteristics, Cause and Practical Issues* (2nd edn). London: Sage.

Brewster, C. and Fager, J. (2000) *Increasing Student Engagement and Motivation: From Time-on-Task to Homework.* Portland, OR: Northwest Regional Educational Laboratory.

BHF (British Heart Foundation) (2017) Physical Inactivity and Sedentary Behaviours Report 2017. Accessed on 09/10/2018 at www.bhf.org.uk/informationsupport/publications/statistics/physical-inactivity-report-2017

Bucek, L.E. (2018) Dance pedagogy for a diverse world: Culturally relevant teaching in theory, research and practice. *Journal of Dance Education 18*, 2, 87–88. doi: 10.1080/15290824.2018.1429189

Capel, S., Leask, M. and Younie, S. (2016) *Starting to Teach in the Secondary School: A Companion to School Experience* (7th edn). Abingdon: Routledge.

Chroinin, D., Fletcher, T. and O'Sullivan, M. (2017) Pedagogical principles of learning to teach meaningful physical education. *Physical Education and Sport Pedagogy 23*, 2, 117–133.

Columna, L., Cook, A., Foley, J.T. and Bailey, J. (2014) Survey development to assess parental satisfaction with adapted physical education teachers' abilities working with children with autism. *Journal Physical Education and Sport Pedagogy 19*, 5, 481–493.

Darling-Hammond, L. (2000) Teacher quality and student achievement: A review of state policy evidence. *Education Policy Analysis Archives 8*, 1, 1–44.

Davies, L. (2017) Making Physical Education Autism-Friendly. *The Association for Physical Education Journal 12*, 3, 53–54.

Department for Education (2013) Teachers' Standards. Guidance for school leaders, school staff and governing bodies. July 2011(introduction updated June 2013). Accessed on 09/10/2018 at https://assets.publishing.service.gov.uk/government/uploads/system/uploads/attachment_data/file/665520/Teachers__Standards.pdf

Department for Education (2014) National curriculum in England: PE programmes of study. Accessed on 09/10/2018 at www.gov.uk/government/publications/national-curriculum-in-england-physical-education-programmes-of-study

Howe, S. and Thornalley, H. (2019) 'The Quest to Determine a Child's Understanding through the Written Feedback Process: With Emphasis on Those Children Assessed as Vulnerable.' In P. Beckley (ed.) *Supporting Vulnerable Children in Early Years: Practical Guidance and Strategies for Working with Children at Risk*. London: Jessica Kingsley Publishers.

IPLA (International Physical Literacy Association) (2017) *International Physical Literacy Association*. Accessed on 02/12/2018 at https://www.physical-literacy.org.uk

Kirk, D. (2011) The crisis of content knowledge. *Physical Education Matters 6*, 2, 34–36.

Law, M., King, G., King, S., Kertoy, M. *et al.*(2006) Patterns of participation in recreational and leisure sctivities among children with complex physical disabilities. *Developmental Medicine and Child Neurology 48*, 5, 337–342.

Lee, J. and Haegele, J.A. (2016) Understanding challenging behaviours of students with autism spectrum disorder in physical education. *Journal of Physical Education, Recreation and Dance 87*, 7, 27–30.

Leekam, S.R., Nieto, C., Libby, S.J., Wing, L. and Gould, J. (2007) Describing the sensory abnormalities of children and adults with autism. *Journal of Autism and Developmental Disorders 37*, 894–910.

Little, H. (2015) Mothers' beliefs about risk and risk-taking in children's outdoor play. *Journal of Adventure Education and Outdoor Learning 15*, 1, 24–39.

Lytle, R., Lavay, B., Robinson, N. and Huettig, C. (2003) Teaching collaboration and consultation skills to preservice adapted physical education teachers. *Journal of Physical Education, Recreation, and Dance 74*, 5, 49–53.

Meckbach, J., Gibbs, B., Almqvist, J. and Quennerstedt, M. (2014) Wii teach movement qualities in physical education. *Sport Science Review 23*, 5–6, 241–266.

Menear, K., and Smith, S. (2011) Teaching physical education to students with autism spectrum disorders: Strategies. *A Journal for Physical and Sport Educators 23*, 3, 21–24.

Mosston, M. and Ashworth, S. (2008) *Teaching Physical Education*. First online edition. Pearson Education. Accessed on 09/10/2018 at www.spectrumofteachingstyles.org/pdfs/ebook/Teaching_Physical_Edu_1st_Online_old.pdf

Pan, C.-Y., Tsai, C.L. and Hsieh, K.W. (2011) Physical activity correlates for children with autism spectrum disorders in middle school physical education. *Research Quarterly for Exercise and Sport 82*, 3, 491–498.

Qi, J. and Ha, A.S. (2012) Inclusion in physical education: A review of literature. *International Journal of Disability, Development and Education 59*, 3, 257–281.

Rosser-Sandt, D.D. and Grey, G.C. (2005) Comparison of physical activity levels between children with and without autistic spectrum disorders. *Adapted Physical Activity Quarterly 22*, 3, 146–159.

Sandt, D. (2013) Social stories for students with autism in physical education. *Journal of Physical Education, Recreation and Dance 79*, 6, 42–45.

Smith, J., Donlan, J. and Smith, B. (2012) *Helping Children with Autism Spectrum Conditions through Everyday Transitions: Small Changes, Big Challenges*. London: Jessica Kingley Publishers.

Shulman, L.S. (1987) Knowledge and teaching: Foundations of the new reform. *Harvard Educational Review 57*, 1, 1–22.

Talbot, M. (2001) Physical Literacy National Conference for Association of Physical Education speech. Cited in Association for Physical Education Health Position Paper 2015. Accessed on 10/10/2018 at www.afpe.org.uk/physical-education/wp-content/uploads/afPE_Health_Position_Paper_Web_Version2015.pdf

Thornalley, H. (2012) Cognitive Dissonance: The dichotomy between conservationism of traditional practice and TGFU facilitation, experienced by Physical Education Undergraduate QTS trainee teachers on teaching placements. International Conference, Teaching Games for Understanding, Oral Presentation, Loughborough University, June 2012.

Thornalley, H. (2015–2018) *Diverse Dance Mix Educational Reports: Trainee Teacher's Role in the Use of Dance Materials within Primary and Secondary Schools*. London: St Mary's University College.

Thornalley, H. (2017) *Main Study: Wimbledon Foundation Early Years Activation Programme Evaluation Report, September 2017*. London and Lincoln: St Mary's University Collegeand Bishop Grosseteste University.

Tinning, R., Kirk, D. and Evans, J. (1993) *Learning to Teach Physical Education*. New York: Prentice Hall.

Weber, A. (2017) Autism, sport and physical activity. Practical strategies to implement in your delivery of sport and physical activity when working with autistic people. *The National Autistic Society*. Accessed on 20/12/2018 at https://www.autism.org.uk/professionals/others/activity-sports.aspx

Whitehead, M. (2010) *Physical Literacy: Throughout the Life Course*. London: Routledge.

WHO (World Health Organization) (2013) *Autism Spectrum Disorders and Other Developmental Disorders: From Raising Awareness to Building Capacity*. Geneva: WHO.

Yianni-Coudurier, C., Darrou, D., Lenoir, P., Verrecchia, B. *et al.* (2008) What clinical characteristics of children with autism influence their inclusion in regular classrooms? *Journal of Intellectual Disability Research*. doi: 10.1111/j.1365-2788.2008.01100.

Chapter Eight

INVOLVING PARENTS

Clare Lawrence

This chapter is written very much from a personal perspective. I cannot, of course, speak for all parents of autistic children; to attempt to do so would be plainly ridiculous given the diversity of individuals that involves. However, I do write after nearly twenty years of working with, talking with and sharing with other parents of autistic children. Together we have spent a great many hours discussing 'what we want' from education for our children, and I think that it is valid to try to enable this collective voice to be heard.

It can be pretty stressful being the parent of an autistic child. Parents are parents to their child all the time: day and night, weekdays and weekends. What's more, this is our child we are talking about. Parents carry all the love, the fear for the future, the hopes and delights, the pride and the disappointments that having a child brings. When you come to understand that your child has autism, many of these emotions will be magnified tenfold. And perhaps the emotion that dominates all the others for us is fear.

I have met a great many parents of autistic children in the years since our son was diagnosed, and I would say that fear is our greatest common denominator. We have found that our child has this strange, unfathomable condition and no one seems to be able to tell us what that will mean for them. Perhaps they have no language. Perhaps, like Sam (my son), they have lots of words but very little communicative ability. They may not turn to you when hurt or upset, may reject physical contact, may experience terrifying meltdowns. What is going to happen to them? How are they ever going to learn to cope 'out there'?

Ultimately it is parents, not schools, that have the responsibility for their child's education. Section 7 of the 1996 Education Act states:

> The parent of every child of compulsory school age shall cause him to receive efficient full-time education suitable—
>
> (a) to his age, ability and aptitude, and
>
> (b) to any special educational needs he may have,
>
> either by regular attendance at school or otherwise.

The duty to meet the autistic needs of the child lies, in law, with that child's parents. Those parents may – indeed most do – decide to try to meet those needs through sending their child to school. Some choose instead to home-educate. If they decide to go down the school route, parents' involvement in that education should never be seen as 'interference'; they have both the right and the responsibility to ensure that their autistic child's 'special education needs' are met.

It is understandable that many parents turn to schools for support. Here are other adults who spend time with, care about and understand your child. Teachers understand child development, and they will be great people, we assume, to help our children in their journey. And this is indeed sometimes the case. We were supported by some wonderful teachers through Sam's education, and I have spoken to a great many parents who have received tremendous kindness, understanding and support from school professionals. But sadly, it is not always so.

According to The National Autistic Society's *School Report 2016*, two thirds of pupils said that their experience of school would be better 'if more teachers understood' and six in ten of the pupils in the survey reported that the worst thing about school, from their perspective, was teachers who do not understand autism. When this lack of understanding in school professionals means that school goes badly for the autistic child, it is the parents who deal with the fall-out. Below are some quotations from parents:

'He would start screaming and throw himself on the floor'

'He stopped eating and sleeping; he lost over a stone in...five weeks'

'He would sit on the same spot, all day long, and not make a noise'

(Kidd and Kaczmarek, 2010, p.262; Lawrence, 2017, p.114; p.104).

Sadly, for many parents of autistic children these desperate situations are the reality. The child screams and clings to the doorpost in the mornings in an attempt to avoid being taken out to the car; they are in constant trouble at school so that all contact with the school is negative; they come home from school exhausted and hostile and take no part in family social activities. Perhaps we as parents should acknowledge just how many days 'off sick' we allow our autistic children to take, just to give them (and us) a break from the misery that is school.

How to make school into a more acceptable, positive environment for autistic pupils is a challenge. Indeed, we need to acknowledge that it may even be a challenge that is impossible to overcome. Mary Warnock, that great advocate for inclusion in education, wrote in 2006 that she agreed with Lorna Wing that for some children with autism there is no such thing as true inclusion in mainstream school. For some, full-time mainstream school by its very nature may be so challenging, exhausting, isolating and downright frightening that they experience no true inclusion at all (Wing, in Cigman, 2006).

In this context, how schools work with the parents of autistic children becomes of paramount importance. Nor is this suggestion made in isolation. During the past ten years, research – both national and international – has concluded that the engagement of parents is vital to the education of all children and young people. The benefits of involving parents in their children's education include 'improved attitudes, behaviour and mental health in children, and increased confidence, satisfaction and interest in parents' (Hornby and Lafaele, 2011, p.39), and engaging with parents to support their children to improve their learning is a key Ofsted requirement. The special educational needs and disabilities (SEND) Code of Practice emphasises the need for schools and parents to work together: 'Where a setting identifies a child as having SEND they must work in partnership with parents to establish the support the child needs' (DfE/DoH 2015, para 5.37); 'Parents should be involved in planning support and, where appropriate, in reinforcing the provision or contributing to progress at home' (para 5.41).

However, what parents want and what schools want are not always the same thing. When I turned to schools for help when Sam was young, what I wanted was help understanding him, understanding how he learned, how to help him to learn more, how to support his interaction and communication. I wanted to understand his autism as a first step to supporting him to understanding it himself. It seemed to me that many of the issues that were of interest regarding other pupils (including our neurotypical daughter) were irrelevant to Sam. As one parent put it, 'For [my son]...being able to know all his colours isn't all that functional. For [him], what is functional is being able to put on his trousers' (Lawrence, 2017, p.161).

The SEND Code of Practice acknowledges something of this friction: 'At times, parents, teachers and others may have differing expectations of how a child's needs are best met'(DfE/DoH 2015, para 1.7). When I talk to parents, their concerns are various and numerous (I am constantly struck by the degree of energy, passion and engagement of these parents, and I remember it acutely from when Sam was younger), but I think they can be summed up fairly simply: parents are concerned when their child is unhappy.

Because of the communication difficulties of autism, it is unlikely that parents of autistic pupils will have a clear understanding of what is going on at school. The autistic pupil, especially after a long and exhausting day at school, is unlikely to rationally and neatly summarise the day for their parents. Instead, that same child may be withdrawn, difficult to reach and challenging behaviourally. Luke Beardon, in Chapter Three, articulately summarises some of the pressures that the autistic pupil faces, and the effect that this can have when that pupil reaches the safety of home. Parents know that their child is unhappy but may be frustrated in knowing exactly why or what could be done to help.

In this situation, the relationship with the school can deteriorate rapidly. It seems to me that there are two common conflicting positions taken between parents of autistic children and school:

1. Parent: My child is unhappy. School: No, they are fine.

2. School: Your child is disruptive. Parent: My child is unhappy.

In neither of these exchanges is communication working efficiently. If the child is 'fine' at school (in other words, is not communicating distress), it can be very difficult for the parent to have their concerns about their child's health and happiness taken seriously. The parent is instead seen as being over-protective or even neurotic. They are seen as creating a problem that doesn't really exist. The other situation, where the child's behaviour is causing the school concern, can be just as damaging. The parents know that the behaviour is communication of distress, but it can be hard for them to be heard. More frequently, the child's behaviour is attributed to 'poor parenting', and there ensues a blame-game which doesn't help anyone.

So – parents want schools to *listen* to them when they discuss their autistic children's needs. This is reasonable, and should be self-evidently good practice, but it is a long way from happening. I recall the passage in John Wyndham's novel *Chocky* where the maths teacher becomes concerned about Matthew's progress. He calls round to Matthew's house unannounced, is invited in by the parents, asked to sit down, invited to discuss his concerns and is even given a glass of whisky. How far we have come since 1968! One school I visited recently had sent out slips to the parents of pupils with SEND (these slips were no doubt lost or never handed on by autistic pupils anyway) that gave an 'opportunity' for a ten-minute consultation to discuss the pupil's progress. These appointment times were inflexible: the parent I spoke to had been given the non-negotiable time of 2.10pm. This time was not convenient for her as a working parent and it was the only opportunity to interact with the SEND team offered by the school during that academic year.

So, parents want to know what is happening to their child at school, and to have their concerns, their input and their expertise regarding that child recognised and acknowledged. However, they also want more than this.

Parents want to have a say in what the education of their autistic children involves and how they access it. Children are at school from the age of 4 to 18 – which is a long time to waste if what they are learning is not relevant to them or when access to learning is being limited. When your child is autistic, you want to know how this learning difference can be overcome so that the child can access the curriculum as successfully as other children. This is the 'reasonable adjustment' that all schools are required to make to prevent discrimination. The autism should not be a barrier to learning.

Parents also want more than for the autism in their child to be 'managed' or 'overcome'. Remediation of learning needs is only part of a successful education for the autistic pupil. The autistic child has a right to understand their own condition, to track their own development, to find ways to accept, understand and indeed celebrate their difference. Pythagorus the Greek philosopher, writing some 2500 years ago, said, 'No one is free who has not obtained the empire of himself. No man is free who cannot command himself' (as quoted in Varle, 1831). Surely, the education of young people with autism should support them to attain this freedom.

Parents are not only required in law to ensure that their children's education is 'efficient' and 'suitable', they are passionate in wanting education to equip their children to be successful adults.

In 2012, The National Autistic Society's review *The Way We Are* (Bancroft *et al.*, 2012) made depressing reading:

- Only 15 per cent of adults with autism are in full-time employment.

- Nearly 40 per cent of adults with autism live at home.

- Sixty-five to 75 per cent rely on family for support needs.

- Seventy-five per cent of adults with autism rely on their parents financially.

Things may have improved in the intervening six years – but then again, they may not have done.

Whatever happens, parents of autistic children are in it for the long haul. All parents remain parents after their children grow up, but most will put down most of the burden of responsibility as their child reaches adulthood. This acceptance that your child has reached independence from you is one of the pains and delights of parenthood. For parents of autistic children, though, the statistics do not look good. Clearly, by the figures suggested above, if the task of education is to enable children to develop into successful, happy and functional adults, it is failing too many of our autistic young people. Sending your autistic child to school and trusting that the system will be effective is simply not working as it should.

Autism is now a compulsory element in ITE. This book goes some way to addressing many of the ways that element can be addressed in a rich and complex way. Through it we can understand the autistic perspective, hear the voice of autistic people and consider issues such as food and sexuality. As educators, each of these is so important, but I would argue further: for each element to be successful, it requires input from and understanding of the parents' perspective. Parents are part of the autism puzzle. It is time that schools recognised the power of their contributions.

Task

What are the parental contact procedures at your school? Do you ring or email parents directly or, for example, send 'praise postcards' or communicate via report card when a pupil is being monitored? Are parents' evenings an opportunity for parents to ask questions, or more an occasion to report back on your pupils' academic progress? What is the protocol for your school reports?

Within these procedures, what opportunities are there for you to discuss concerns about an individual pupil, or to ask questions of parents about the ways to communicate with autistic pupils? How would parents of an autistic pupil communicate with you directly if they had a concern?

We live in a modern age of effective communication: how could you enable more effective communication around autistic pupils that you teach? Design some protocols for you to communicate with parents/carers or for them to communicate with you around such issues as a change in classroom routine, an upcoming school trip, illness in the family, the death of a pet, homework concerns and so on.

References

Bancroft, K., Batten, A., Lambert, S. and Madders, T. (2012) *The Way We Are: Autism in 2012*. London: The National Autistic Society.

Cigman, R. (ed.) (2006) *Included or Excluded?: The Challenge of the Mainstream for Some SEN Children*. London: Routledge.

DfE/DoH (2015) Special Educational Needs and Disability Code of Practice: 0 to 25 Years. Statutory Guidance for Organisations Which Work With and Support Children and Young People Who Have Special Educational Needs or Disabilities. Accessed on 03/10/2018 at www.gov.uk/government/publications/send-code-of-practice-0-to-25

Hornby, G. and Lafaele, R. (2011) Barriers to parental involvement in education: An explanatory model. *Educational Review 63*, 1, 37–52.

Kidd, T. and Kaczmarek, E. (2010) The experiences of mothers home educating their children with autism spectrum disorder. *Issues in Educational Research 20*, 3, 257–275.

Lawrence, C. (2017) Can sharing education between home and school benefit the child with autism? Doctoral dissertation, Sheffield Hallam University.

NAS (The National Autistic Society) (2016) *School Report 2016*. London: The National Autistic Society. Accessed on 03/10/2018 at www.autism.org.uk/schoolreport2016

Wyndham, J. (1968) *Chocky*. London: Penguin Books.

Chapter Nine

'I CAN'T EAT THAT, I DON'T LIKE IT...'

Recognising and Responding to Mealtime Challenges Associated with Autism

Jo Cormack

Approximately three quarters of autistic children have problems with eating (Ledford and Gast, 2006). Despite this statistic, rather than interpreting limited or 'picky'[1] eating through the lens of autism, anecdotal evidence suggests that many professionals default to a culturally accepted narrative that food fussiness is 'just a phase' which children will eventually grow out of.

Dismissing picky eating as a transient stage in neurotypical children's development is problematic. However, for autistic children – for whom food selectivity can persist into adolescence (Nadon *et al.*, 2011) – ignoring food-rejecting behaviours (or worse still, seeing

---

1   Although 'picky eating' is a problematic term because it implies wilful choosiness, it is the phrase employed by parents and academics and so will be used in this chapter.

them as 'naughty') leads to significant lost opportunities to meet children's needs.

Any discussion of how to support autistic children must be underpinned by the acknowledgement that every autistic person is an individual with their own needs and strengths. However, there may also be categories of experiencing which many autistic children have in common. This tension between seeing the individual and recognising shared responses to the world is perfectly illustrated by the subject of eating. No two autistic children will respond to food in the same way for the same reasons, but certain features of autism can make eating a varied diet very hard:

- gastrointestinal issues

- the social side of meals

- the sensory aspects of eating

- anxiety

- behavioural rigidity.

Gastrointestinal issues

The likelihood of an autistic child experiencing frequent gastrointestinal complaints (including food sensitivity, bloating, diarrhoea and constipation) is triple that of their neurotypical peers, with constipation and diarrhoea being especially common (Chaidez, Hansen and Hertz-Picciotto, 2014). Perhaps the limited diet typical of autistic children contributes to these digestive problems, or maybe negative associations with food due to physical discomfort are a factor in the development of food aversions. Perhaps – as is often the case – there is an interplay of factors.

The social side of meals

Meal and snack times in a school setting are full of interpersonal challenges. Sometimes, the overwhelming nature of the communal eating environment can lead to autistic children simply not eating while away from the family home. One study – comparing autistic children with their neurotyopical siblings – found that 37.5 per cent of the autistic siblings did not eat in settings including restaurants, school and day care, compared to 8.3 per cent of the neurotypical siblings (Nadon *et al.*, 2011).

All of the tiny decisions and micro-interactions that characterise meal times can be hard for children who find it difficult to read social cues. Equally, in some educational settings, there is only a short time allocated to meals; pressure to eat fast can be very anxiety-provoking for some autistic children.

These social demands are difficult in and of themselves but coupled with an environment that is overwhelming from a sensory perspective, they can simply be too much for some autistic children. For most of us, eating is a relatively automatic process; we may not be especially affected by the sense data received and processed by our brains as we consume our food. This is often not the case for those on the autism spectrum. Sensory processing difficulties will be explored in the subsequent section of this chapter.

Task 9.1

Working in small groups, think about which senses we use when we eat. Can you list them and think of an example for each? *Example: Sight – we see the colour and shape of the food on the plate.*

You will probably have considered the well-known 'five senses' but actually, we have eight:

- **Tactile** – this is the sense of touch

- **Visual** – this refers to sight

- **Auditory** – this refers to hearing

- **Gustatory** – this is the sense of taste

- **Olfactory** – this is the sense of smell

- **Vestibular** – this sense relates to balance and movement. It allows us to know where we are in space

- **Proprioceptive** – this sense has to do with our awareness of our bodies, especially where body parts are in relation to one another

- **Interoceptive** – this sense lets us know what is happening inside our bodies – if we are hungry or need to use the toilet, for example.

Q: Which of the above do we use when eating?
A: All of them!

Task 9.2

To learn more about sensory perception and autism, read:

Bogdashina, O. (2016) *Sensory Perceptual Issues in Autism and Asperger Syndrome: Different Sensory Experiences – Different Perceptual Worlds*. London: Jessica Kingsley Publishers.

To learn more about sensory integration, read:

Ayres, A.J. and Robbins, J. (2005) *Sensory Integration and the Child: Understanding Hidden Sensory Challenges*. Western Psychological Services.

Sensory processing

Sensory processing difficulties are a key feature of autism. Researchers found that more than 90 per cent of autistic children had 'sensory abnormalities' in multiple domains (Leekam *et al.*, 2007, p.903). This has many implications for eating: autistic children may be under-responsive in some sensory domains and over-responsive in others, with a sub-set being both under- and over-responsive (Cermak, Curtin and Bandini, 2010).

Over-responsiveness can lead to oral aversions where a child is highly sensitive to how certain textures feel in the mouth. An over-responsive child may react strongly to smells, maybe gagging or retching. Under-responsiveness can lead to sensory-seeking behaviours, such as 'pocketing' or keeping food in the cheeks.

While the food on the plate presents one set of sensory challenges, the communal eating environment presents another. It is often filled with loud noises and strong smells and is likely to be full of movement and colour. There is an awful lot to contend with before a child has even sat down to eat.

Anxiety

Children on the autism spectrum often experience high levels of anxiety, sometimes to a degree that significantly interferes with day-to-day functioning. This can be interpreted as a response to some of the characteristics associated with autism, such as difficulty with social interaction or sensory sensitivity (Rodgers *et al.*, 2016).

In relation to food, if an autistic child has had many negative mealtime experiences, they may come to dread meals and snacks. Anxiety and stress have a negative impact on appetite and this can quickly develop into a pattern where a child is worried about eating and so they no longer feel hungry, thus making eating harder still.

Behavioural rigidity

Routine is extremely important to many autistic children. It has been suggested that this need for things to be the same may be a way of coping with anxiety (Grahame *et al.*, 2015). This makes a lot of sense when we consider the sensory challenges inherent in food: if a child finds eating hard, clinging to the familiar and predictable may make them feel psychologically safer.

In an educational setting, especially one where children are not able to bring in food from home, meals and snacks may not always be the same. Some autistic children become attached to certain utensils or have 'rules' about how foods are prepared or presented. What is possible to accommodate in the home environment may not be feasible at school. This can present problems for staff and children alike.

Task 9.3 Trying to understand the need for control

It can be hard to imagine what it is like to need things to be the same. In order to simulate food-related anxiety borne of not being in control during an eating scenario, try the following exercise:

You will need:

- foods (see below)

- a blindfold (a scarf would work well)

- lots of teaspoons.

Working in groups of three, one person is 'the child' (C), one 'the observer' (O) and the third, 'the adult' (A). In advance, check that the person being the child does not have any food allergies, intolerances or strong food dislikes.

A blindfolds C then hands them a spoon with a foodstuff on. There will be three foods:

1. plain yoghurt (make sure you have refrigeration facilities to store this safely before the exercise!)

2. cereal (any with no added sugar) crumbled into a powder

3. panko (or other crunchy) breadcrumbs soaked in a little soy sauce.

These are increasingly odd and hard to recognise for C.

A gives C a teaspoonful of each of the three foods to eat, one by one.

O records how C responds – do they hesitate? Grimace? Laugh nervously? Recoil?

After tasting all three teaspoons of food, C should tell A and O how it felt to be asked to eat something they had not previously identified and did not know whether they were comfortable with.

Next, take the blindfold off and invite C to try the three foods again, in any order. Ask them to answer the following questions:

1. Can you describe how (and if) you experienced things differently when you had a little more control, due to being more familiar with the tastes and more able to predict and recognise them?

2. Did it make any difference to you that you were in control of the order you ate the foods the second time around? If so, how?

Finally, the group nominates a spokesperson to report back to the large group. They will share their reflections on what it might be like to feel out of control and anxious about a sensory experience which is new and hard to predict.

It is useful to note that it is not only children on the autism spectrum who are neophobic (anxious about unfamiliar foods). To help any child build their confidence in relation to eating, an empathic and exploratory stance is of paramount importance. This is where the goal is to try to understand what the experience of eating is like for the child, rather than making assumptions about how food 'should be' experienced.

Implications for practice

Food can feature in the classroom in many ways besides meal and snack time. For example, in primary education and early years, younger children may engage in sensory or 'messy' play and in secondary education, food technology will be on the curriculum. These activities can be extremely hard for some autistic children to engage with.

It can be difficult for practitioners to understand the extent of some children's food anxiety. They may not appreciate that just touching the sticky surface of a chopped fruit or being in a food-tech lab where there are strong smells from a previous lesson can be almost impossible to tolerate.

Task 9.4

Drawing on what you have learned, what practical strategies in the classroom or dining hall might support autistic children who are anxious about food?

Here are some suggestions to explore with students following the discussion:

- Spend time speaking with the child (if they are verbal) and their parent or carer to get an in-depth understanding of how they relate to food. Do they find smells hard? Do they struggle with communal eating? Without this knowledge it is very hard to know how to be supportive.

- Adapt activities for autistic pupils so they can still engage with the curriculum, using support staff if appropriate. For example, a child who has a high degree of tactile sensitivity and is anxious about touching chopped fruit may still be able to take part in the food technology lesson where fruit salad is being prepared. They could perhaps use latex gloves, cocktail sticks (if safe) or have a teaching assistant to 'be their hands'. Strategies like these will enable the child to enjoy making the fruit salad while benefiting from pressure-free exposures to non-preferred foods.

- Explore adaptations to the eating environment. Some children may need a quiet room away from crowds, loud noises and strong smells where they can eat their meal with a friend. Perhaps a child may be allowed to go into the dining area early and choose their food before it gets busy. Small changes like this can make a big difference.

- Never pressure an autistic (or neurotypical) child to eat or try a food they are not comfortable with. This will raise anxiety and make eating worse. Although it is culturally normal to encourage children to 'eat up' or try something new, this is neither an effective nor a supportive strategy.

- There may be times when it is necessary, in conjunction with the head or your line manager, to consider making exceptions to school policy in order to be inclusive. For example, some schools have 'lunch box rules', which an autistic child's accepted foods may not meet. That child needs to be able to bring in food they can eat in order to learn and thrive. Failure to meet this need is a failure to be inclusive.

- The core goal for teachers should be to foster positive and low-anxiety interactions with food rather than pushing children to do things they are not comfortable with. This prioritisation of long-term over short-term goals is what will help children gain in confidence with their eating.

Summary

- There are many reasons why children on the autism spectrum may find eating and interacting with food difficult.

- In order to support autistic children, these difficulties need to be understood and empathised with.

- Every autistic child will have their own unique relationship with food and some will have no eating issues at all. It is important to avoid making assumptions and take time to get to know the child as an individual.

- Practitioners need to question cultural norms, such as seeing eating a varied diet as 'good behaviour'. Building confidence and reducing anxiety should be prioritised over persuading children to eat or interact with foods they are wary of.

- It is appropriate to make adaptations to the school rules and environment in order to include autistic pupils.

References

Cermak, S.A., Curtin, C. and Bandini, L.G. (2010) Food selectivity and sensory sensitivity in children with autism spectrum disorders. *Journal of the American Dietetic Association 110*, 2, 238–246.

Chaidez, V., Hansen, R.L. and Hertz-Picciotto, I. (2014) Gastrointestinal problems in children with autism, developmental delays or typical development. *Journal of Autism and Developmental Disorders 44*, 5, 1117–1127.

Grahame, V., Brett, D., Dixon, L., McConachie, H. *et al.* (2015) Managing repetitive behaviours in young children with autism spectrum disorder (ASD): Pilot randomised controlled trial of a new parent group intervention. *Journal of Autism and Developmental Disorders 45*, 10, 3168–3182.

Ledford, J.R. and Gast, D.L. (2006) Feeding problems in children with autism spectrum disorders: A review. *Focus on Autism and Other Developmental Disabilities 21*, 3, 153–166.

Leekam, S.R., Nieto, C., Libby, S.J., Wing, L. and Gould, J. (2007) Describing the sensory abnormalities of children and adults with autism. *Journal of Autism and Developmental Disorders 37*, 5, 894–910.

Nadon, G., Feldman, D.E., Dunn, W. and Gisel, E. (2011) Mealtime problems in children with Autism Spectrum Disorder and their typically developing siblings: A comparison study. *Autism 15*, 1, 98–113.

Rodgers, J., Wigham, S., McConachie, H., Freeston, M., Honey, E. and Parr, J.R. (2016) Development of the anxiety scale for children with autism spectrum disorder (ASC-ASD): Measuring anxiety in ASD. *Autism Research 9*, 11, 1205–1215.

Chapter Ten

RELATIONSHIPS AND SEX EDUCATION IN AUTISM

Jan Hargrave and Jo Tasker

If you ask someone when they learnt about relationships and sex, the very best answer they could give is that they have always known. Ideally learning about the 'birds and bees' should not be an embarrassing single exchange between adult and child, but a frank, open and ongoing discussion where topics arise, and questions are answered, in an age-appropriate way.

In our experience, although there are some who are doing some great work, relationships and sex education in schools is still poorly delivered. In primary schools a 'puberty talk' may be fitted in between SATs and the end of term, the content being the same year after year, and at secondary level someone may be invited into school to demonstrate to pupils how to put a condom on a cucumber and deliver a brief talk about sexually transmitted infections. In neither case is this fitted into the context of relationships.

For most people when reflecting on how they learnt about sex and relationships, the learning was through osmosis, picked up from their peer group. Inevitably, this can lead to misunderstanding and misrepresentation; the myths associated with this topic are still the same today as they were 50 years ago. Experimentation also plays a part during adolescence, but to do this safely young people need to understand risks, boundaries, appropriate and inappropriate behaviour, and those more theoretical concepts such as consent.

For autistic pupils the relationship and sex education (RSE) sessions may be fraught with challenge. Sadly, the 'one size fits all' nature of the delivery of these sessions, and the time pressures felt by schools which limit flexibility of delivery, mean that the additional needs of these pupils are seldom considered as carefully as they should be. Autistic individuals have as much – arguably more – need of this education as do their peers, so it is essential that their needs be accommodated. This chapter aims to address some of the ways that the needs of autistic pupils can be met in RSE delivery.

The context

The Children and Social Work Act (2017) requires the Secretary of State to introduce statutory relationships education in all primary schools, and sex education for all secondary schools including special schools, in September 2019. This includes maintained, academies, special and independent schools.

Schools should ensure that students with SEND in mainstream schools receive sex and relationships education. Teachers may find that they have to be more explicit and plan work in different ways in order to meet the individual needs of children with SEND.

For RSE in autism to be effective, the ground needs to be prepared and ideally parents need to be involved. Care needs to be taken that this 'education' does not in fact further confuse the autistic pupil, or place them in danger by presenting ambiguous suggestions or messages that they could misconstrue and which could lead to difficulty in real-life situations. Equally, after an RSE session, most pupils will have the 'decompression' of discussion with their peers; autistic pupils may not have access to this in the same way. They may also pick up confusing and contradictory messages during this time, so it is essential to allow for follow-up (from a mentor, form teacher, TA and/or their parents) as part of the process.

Prepare yourself first

The place to start in preparing to deliver effective RSE to all pupils is with yourself. Think about your own attitudes and vulnerabilities; be clear about your boundaries. How will your own attitudes and values – and we all have them – impact on what you will speak about? Are you confident to deliver the session or do you need training to equip yourself with the necessary skills? It is OK to admit embarrassment to yourself, but you need a way to overcome this if it is not to impact on the content and delivery of your teaching.

Ideally RSE should be delivered as part of an integrated, spiral curriculum, where RSE is embedded across all subjects. Every school should have an RSE policy which outlines the values and ethos of the school in relation to RSE and how they wish this to be delivered. The RSE policy should include the voice of pupils and parents. This forms an agreement between you and your senior management team about what is delivered and how it is delivered.

Task 10.1

Consider what you would need in an RSE policy to ensure that you feel supported to deliver RSE content.

If a pupil asks a sensitive question which falls outside the remit of the lesson, do you know how to respond? Many policies will leave this to the discretion of the teacher by using terms like 'honestly, and openly' regarding your response. What does this mean? What are the dangers if you get the tone of your answer wrong?

Good practice suggests that a robust RSE policy should:

- describe the ethos of the school in relation to RSE

- define RSE – aims and objectives

- describe how RSE is provided and who is responsible for providing it

- describe how staff will be trained

- describe how equality, inclusion and differentiated learning will be ensured

- say how RSE is monitored and evaluated and how pupil learning is assessed

- explain clearly how to answer those 'sensitive' questions

- say how children thought to be at risk will be supported

- reflect the views of parents and pupils and how they will be involved

- include information about parents' right to withdraw their child from the non-statutory elements of RSE (science)

- include a review date

- describe how the policy links to others.

Setting the rules

It is important before you start an RSE session to ensure a safe environment for everyone by being clear about issues of confidentiality and the sharing of sensitive information. This is true for all pupils, but autistic young people may need these rules to be made even more explicit.

The RSE lesson may prompt a change in the timetable, which itself may be an issue for autistic pupils. This may or may not include a change in the teacher timetabled to deliver at that time – again, this needs to be made clear to the pupils in advance.

More problematic is that the rules of what can, and what cannot, be discussed in an RSE lesson. The maths or English teacher rarely brings up the words penis and vagina, nor will it be acceptable to use these words – or the alternatives about to be discussed – in future lessons. For the autistic pupil it should be made clear that these things will be discussed in this lesson (and can be discussed one to one with the pastoral team around that child if they seek further information) but have not now become acceptable to use in other subject lessons. Nor is disclosure regarding the subjects discussed in this lesson something to be continued out of the classroom; autistic pupils need to be told explicitly about discussion of the subjects raised in this lesson once the lesson has finished – it may not be appropriate, for example, to share information about your periods with the bus driver.

It is also essential that you as the teacher for the session are absolutely confident about the boundaries of confidentiality and how a safeguarding disclosure will be managed.

Good quality RSE should start in early years and evolve as the child journeys through adolescence, preparing them for transition into adulthood. The messages we give all children should be of a consistent quality, delivered age appropriately and often led by the child. For autistic pupils this should be tailored to fit that young person taking into account their sensory requirements, emotional understanding and sexual identity (Franklin, Raws and Smeaton, 2015).

Language

It is imperative that we consider in advance the language that we will use during RSE lessons. What are your personal boundaries? Are there words you are not happy to use or hear? How will you make it clear to the pupils where the boundaries are, and how they are different in this session? Remember that this information needs to be made explicitly to autistic pupils. It is manifestly unjust if an autistic pupil is punished for labelling a diagram of the urinary system with 'prick' in a biology lesson because the different uses of terminology in different context has not be taught explicitly.

Task 10.2

Complete the list below, only including words with which you feel at ease in a professional setting. Discuss your list with your group. Are there some words on your list that others find offensive or inappropriate, and vice versa? Are some words and terms unfamiliar to you? Consider also how many of the terms have a dual meaning.

NB this is *not* an activity that it is advisable to undertake in this form with pupils, although it may be adapted (see below).

Penis willy, cock, prick, knob, dick

Vagina

Breasts tits, boobs

Testicles balls

Scrotum

Vulva

Nipples

Erection hard-on, stiffy

Ejaculation come

Orgasm

Masturbation

Pregnancy

Menstruation period

Pubic hair bush

This list helps us to appreciate two things. One is our own levels of embarrassment and discomfort. Do we find some words distasteful or threatening? How are we going to manage our own comfort/ discomfort in a classroom situation? The second issue that the list identifies is just how confusing this language could be for someone with autism. A knob is also a door handle, a bush is a plant and a tit a small yellow and blue bird. In America, a period is a full stop. There are issues of register to be considered too. It is acceptable to say that the ball hit you in the testicles, but you may be reprimanded for telling your teacher you have been hit in the balls. In most primary schools, children are taught that the only acceptable terms are those that are biologically correct, which works if we are teaching them which words to use when visiting their doctor but will not adequately equip them to fit into their peer group and may increase the likelihood of bullying.

When delivering RSE you will need to decide on the language you are happy to use, and to ascertain the language that the young people are familiar with. You could ask them to sort some words – of your choosing – into those they use at home, words they use at school or when we visit the doctor, and words they might use with their peer group. Part of this discussion is likely to include which words have been omitted and why. They might consider which words might be offensive and to whom, and which words they would choose not to use. This clarity should support autistic pupils, although you will need to monitor the discussion carefully to ensure that they are not being 'set up' by peers to believe that hard-core words are innocuous.

Bear in mind also that autism can include a propensity for literal translation. Monitor the language that you use to avoid misinterpretation and needless anxiety:

Teacher: A boy's testicles will drop.

(*Pupil*: What, off?)

Teacher: A boy's voice will break.

(*Pupil*: Does it hurt? Can it be mended?)

Puberty

Puberty is a time of fundamental change, and many autistic people find change difficult. If puberty is a time of instability for all young people, for people with autism it can be seismic. Temple Grandin describes puberty (2006):

> Puberty can be hell. It is all so scary, frightening, causing meltdowns for boys, having erections, wet dreams. The worst thing was pubic hair, so scratchy – I made it so sore, it started bleeding there, I really wanted to pull out the pubic hair.

In terms of RSE, the 'puberty talk' is usually delivered in Year 5 and/or 6. This is a time of great change in body and emotions and The Talk is often approached by children with some degree of trepidation, excitement and anxiety. It should include that bodies come in all shapes and sizes, go through puberty at different times, grow at different rates, and this is all perfectly normal. Unfortunately, this lack of specificity can exacerbate autistic anxiety. Changes cannot be planned for accurately and there is a lamentable lack of specificity. 'Everyone is different', we argue – but this is unlikely to reassure the autistic pupil.

A sensible approach for autistic young people is to concentrate on the scientific. Every body part, both internal and external, has a name and a function. Some body parts produce fluids including urine, semen, sweat and blood. Understanding where the fluids are produced, why and when can be reassuring. Be cautious, though, as some autistic pupils may have a propensity to collect facts about puberty and will need sensitivity regarding awareness of who these facts should be shared and when. Research indicates that when collecting these facts, the most likely source of information, if schools do not provide it, is internet pornography (Martellozzo et al., 2016). It is essential that young people with autism have a trusted source for facts, and a trusted ear for the disclosure of interesting facts discovered, in school or at home (or both). 'Shutting down' these safe avenues may put the pupil into far greater danger.

Relationships

The relationships aspect of RSE is just as important as the sex part, and arguably may be the greater challenge for autistic pupils. Relationships begin with establishing friendships, which in teenage years rely on having an understanding of complex interactions, body language and facial expressions. Isolation of autistic pupils may become more pronounced as social rules become more complex around puberty. This aspect of RSE requires a more targeted approach for autistic pupils than may be necessary for their neurotypical peers: Mere exposure to appropriate, social situations does not help a child with autism improve their social skills, or there would not be a problem in the first place (Jordan and Jones, 1999). It is not as simple as approaching someone in the street and asking them to be your friend. Successful interaction relies on shared interests, initiation of conversation, and an interest (or ability to feign interest) in what the other person is talking about. The child with autism may only be engaged if talking about one special passion and find it very hard to participate in conversation if the topic does not interest them. As Wendy Lawson says: 'It would be easy for other people to read my lack of attentiveness as rudeness, laziness, inability to share an interest or even sheer snobbery. However, actually it's my being "attention tunnelled" or monotrophic' (Lawson, 2003, p.22).

Support for autistic pupils with social skills should, it is hoped, be provided additionally and you are unlikely to be able to provide the level or complexity of support required during your RSE lessons. However, it is important that you are aware and that the information that you give during these sessions does not further confuse autistic pupils or put undue pressure on them.

Intimacy

For those children journeying through puberty and entering adolescence the next emotional milestone is potentially entering into a more intimate relationship, whether this is heterosexual or homosexual. Realistically, in today's digitalised world many young people will meet through social media. Young people with autism may find internet communication easier than face-to-face communication as there is usually a use of consistent and easily recognisable emoticons which replaces the need to decode people's body language, facial expressions and vocal tone. It also provides opportunities for learning through repetition that supports children who take longer to learn new things and embeds the learning they do in the classroom by undertaking activities as many times as they need to (Cerebra, 2015). Part of responsible RSE should be clear and open discussion around internet safety. Autistic pupils may be vulnerable to exploitation, and to naïve sharing of inappropriate images.

When discussing online dating protocols and etiquette, the most useful source for you as the RSE deliverer is likely to be the other pupils. They will be up to date about what is, and what is not, current in a way that teachers are unlikely to be. Collect the group's collective advice together and create a list of Dos and Don'ts agreed by the class. Explicit rules such as these can be invaluable for the autistic pupil.

Approaching someone in 'real life' can be more of a challenge for autistic young people. The concept of 'flirting' is almost impossible to describe as it has so many manifestations. It can be easy for a young person with autism to misread gestures of friendship or kindness as flirting, and consequently to respond inappropriately. It may also be that a young person with autism makes an individual their special interest. If the subject of that interest is someone in the public domain – a musician or actor, for example – this can actually increase social inclusion, particularly amongst girls. An encyclopaedic knowledge of the personal lives of the latest K-pop band may enable an autistic pupil to join in with peer discussions. On the other hand, if the subject of interest is a real person – a peer or a teacher – there is a real danger that the autistic person's interest will tip over into behaviour regarded as stalking. As with so much, there are unwritten rules about how much it is 'OK' to know about different people. It is not surprising that autistic people find the concept of romantic or sexual relationships so challenging.

Consent

One of the most important elements of RSE for all pupils is the issue of consent. Teaching children about consent plays a vital part in meeting schools' safeguarding requirements and fits within the social, moral, spiritual and cultural obligations expected and measured by Ofsted. More importantly, it is essential that all young people understand the issue of consent in order to keep themselves and others safe. Good RSE supports a very strong consent message from modelling behaviours in early years, to supporting children to ask for, and receive a consensual message as they develop their relationships. For children who have difficulties with understanding facial expression or body language the safest advice is 'I will not touch someone without asking them first' and 'just because someone hasn't said no doesn't mean they have said yes' and 'no means no'. These messages needs to be constantly re-iterated with opportunities to practice in various situations.

Task 10.3

Consider the explicit advice given below regarding 'Saying No'. Discuss the message being delivered here as the 'bottom line'.

- Breathe deeply.

- Stand up straight and look the other person in the eyes (if you feel comfortable doing so).

- Say 'no' loudly and clearly.

- Look serious: no smiling, no laughing.

- Push a hand forward, hard, as if pushing the person away.

Task 10.4

Visit the National Autistic Society website[1] to see advice on RSE and autism from Lynne Moxon.

Visit the TES website[2] to read tips by Lynn McCann on making sex education more autism friendly.

Sexual and gender identity

Research suggests that individuals on the autism spectrum report increased homosexuality, bisexuality and asexuality, but decreased heterosexuality (George and Stokes, 2018). A child on the spectrum may not invest in binary gender identities as they may not be constrained by social messages of sexuality and sexual expression. They may be less likely to suppress same sex attractions and their relationship are often more fluid. This is not without its difficulties as others may not believe or understand the child. The child with autism is more likely to be androgynous, choosing to express themselves sexually in a way that is seen as non-heteronormative, such as pansexual, intersex, asexual or questioning (George and Stokes, 2018). Issues of autism and gender identity are explored in more depth in Chapter Eleven.

Ensure that your approach to RSE does not leave anyone out or make anyone feel different or inadequate. It is also important to emphasise that having a sexual relationship is a matter of

---

1   www.autism.org.uk/about/communication/sex-education/top-tips.aspx
2   https://www.tes.com/news/eight-ways-make-sex-education-autism-friendly

personal choice. Peer pressure and media input can make young people believe that sexual relationships are compulsory. One autistic girl told me that she 'had' to have a boyfriend by the time she was 16 in order to 'be normal'. It is important in RSE to combat these pressures and to reassure all young people that it is perfectly acceptable to make a decision not to be sexually active, either at the current time or at any time.

The spectrum of sexuality is as diverse as the autistic spectrum. The aim is to ensure your RSE programme is as inclusive as possible. It needs to address homophobic and transphobic bullying to ensure that all children, including those with autism, are fully protected. Ensure that space is given for people to hear, use and understand the words 'gay', 'lesbian', 'bisexual' and 'transgender'. It is also imperative that the young person understands that there is a risk that they will experience homophobic bullying and is taught resilience strategies to meet the challenges that unfortunately still exist within society (Abbott and Howarth, 2005).

Assessment of RSE and ongoing support for you as teacher

Finally, underpinning the RSE scheme of work is robust pre- and post-delivery assessment. To deliver a robust scheme of work which relates to that cohort of young people, assessment and evaluation should inform current and future delivery. Although young people do not fail or succeed in RSE at school, they should have opportunities to explore their attitudes and values and reflect on their behaviours. This should happen within a safe and supportive environment that gives all young people the space to discuss, challenge and explore potentially sensitive topics.

Assessment of RSE input should be pertinent for all children but should additionally be tailored specifically to the needs of autistic pupils. Have they understood the content of the lesson? Were the resources used appropriate? Was there opportunity for conversation with parents, pastoral support or the SENDco so the topic can be reinforced at home? With the autistic pupil there should never be an attitude of 'job done' regarding this subject. RSE education will need to go on in more detail, and for longer, with autistic young people than with their peers. If they are to be safe and to have the chance to be confident in their own sexuality, much support may be needed into the future for some time.

Embedding RSE in a school curriculum is challenging. The pressure to deliver the core subjects means that often RSE slips off the timetable or the job is left to parents who can sometimes feel ill equipped. This can leave all children, particularly those embarking on transition to secondary, vulnerable and confused. Add to this the vulnerability associated with being autistic with its attendant propensity to misunderstand and misinterpret and the journey through adolescence into adulthood can be frightening and at times dangerous. However, with the support of an enlightened teacher helping to navigate the way, with the right information and guidance, young people including those with autism will be able to have (or not have) the relationships of their choice.

Further reading

Attwood, S. (2008) *Making Sense of Sex: A Forthright Guide to Puberty, Sex and Relationships for People with Asperger's Syndrome.* London: Jessica Kingsley Publishers.

Attwood, T., Hénault, I. and Dubin, N. (2014) *The Autism Spectrum, Sexuality and the Law: What Every Parent and Professional Needs to Know.* London: Jessica Kingsley Publishers.

Buron, K.D. (2007) *A 5 Is Against the Law! Social Boundaries: Straight Up!* Shawnee Mission, KS: Autism Asperger Publishing Company.

Cerebra (2015) *Learning Disabilities, Autism and Internet Safety: A Parent's Guide.* Camarthen: Cerebra.

Davies, C. and Dubie, M. (2012) *Intimate Relationships and Sexual Health: A Curriculum for Teaching Adolescents/Adults with High Functioning ASD and Other Social Challenges.* Shawnee Mission, KS: AAPC Publishing.

Family Planning Association (n.d.) *Periods: What You Need to Know.* Accessed on 04/10/2018 at www.fpa.org.uk/sites/default/files/periods-what-you-need-to-know.pdf

Hartman, D. (2015) *The Growing up Guide for Girls: What Girls on the Autism Spectrum Need to Know!* London: Jessica Kingsley Publishers.

Hartman, D. (2015) *The Growing up Book for Boys: What Boys on the Autism Spectrum Need to Know!* London: Jessica Kingsley Publishers.

Reynolds, K.E. (2015) *What's Happening to Ellie? A Book about Puberty for Girls and Young Women with Autism and Related Conditions.* London: Jessica Kingsley Publishers.

Reynolds, K.E. (2014) *What's Happening to Tom? A Book about Puberty for Boys and Young Men with Autism and Related Conditions.* London: Jessica Kingsley Publishers.

Ripley, K. (2014) *Exploring Friendships, Puberty and Relationships: A Programme to Help Children and Young People on the Autism Spectrum Cope with the Challenges of Adolescence.* London: Jessica Kingsley Publishers.

Wrobel, M. (2003) *Taking Care of Myself: A Hygiene, Puberty and Personal Curriculum for Young People with Autism.* Arlington, TX: Future Horizons.

References

Abbott, D. and Howarth, J. (2005) *Secret Loves, Hidden Lives? Exploring Issues for People with Learning Disabilities who are Gay, Lesbian and Bisexual.* London: Policy Press.

Cerebra (2015) *Learning Disabilities, Autism and Internet Safety: A Parent's Guide.* Camarthen: Cerebra.

Franklin, A., Raws, P. and Smeaton, E. (2015) *Unprotected, Overprotected: Meeting the Needs of Young People with Learning Disabilities Who Experience, or Are at Risk of, Sexual Exploitation.* Ilford: Barnardo's.

Gender Matters NCB (2018) https://www.anti-bullyingalliance.org.uk/gender-matters-training-resources-secondary-schools

George. R and Stokes M.A (2018) Sexual orientation in Autism Spectrum Disorder. *Autism Research 11*, 133–141. doi: 10.1002/aur.1892 VC 2017

Grandin, T. (2006) *Stress and Coping in Autism.* New York: Oxford University Press.

Jordan, R. and Jones, G. (1999) Review of research into educational interventions for children with autism in the UK. *Autism 3*, 1, 101–110.

Lawson, W. (2003) *Build Your Own Life: A Self-Help Guide for Individuals with Asperger Syndrome.* London: Jessica Kingsley Publishers.

Martellozzo, E., Monaghan, A., Adler, J.R., Davidson, J. *et al.* (2016) *I Wasn't Sure It Was Normal to Watch It.* London: NSPCC.

Chapter Eleven

AUTISM AND GENDER FLUIDITY

Practical Suggestions for Thinking about Gender Fluidity in Pupils with Autism

Lyndsay Muir

Why are we looking at this?

The rationale for this chapter is that there are a significant number of autistic people for whom the question of gender identity is a co-occurrence. According to figures from the Centre of Expertise on Gender Dysphoria, VU University Medical Centre, Amsterdam, almost 10 per cent of the referred children and adolescents present with autism (de Vries *et al.*, 2010, cited in Bouman and Arcelus, 2018). This prevalence is ten times more than would be expected based on the diagnostic prevalence rate of autism amongst the whole population, thought to be around 1 per cent or less. Expressed in simple terms, a noteworthy proportion of autistic young people are also trans (i.e. their gender identity does not match their assigned sex at birth). As yet, there is little evidence to support theories as to why this may be the case, with hypotheses ranging from pre-natal exposure to testosterone, rigid thinking that leaves little room for being a 'tomboyish girl' or a 'feminine boy', together with a suggestion that a sense of 'being different' could be experienced as gender dysphoria. As teachers we are gifted with the professional task of meeting the needs of all pupils, so such speculations are immaterial, whereas the presence of pupils with diverse identities is a reality.

So, what we can say is that it is quite likely that teachers will encounter pupils who may co-experience both autism and some degree of gender ambiguity. With both a strong vocational desire to meet the needs of all pupils and a requirement to achieve this as a professional standard, gender ambiguity in pupils with autism is thus worthy of our attention. Whilst there are and will continue to be autistic young people in schools, a significant percentage of whom will also experience issues around gender identity (and in a related but distinct way, sexuality too), there will also be trans and non-binary pupils who are not autistic. We know that these groups intersect and overlap and we also know that a lack of a medical diagnosis does not mean that such diversity and individual need is not present. Better practice, perhaps, to assume that there are gender-questioning and autistic young people in our teaching groups, whether they are formally identified and visible to us as educators or not.

Thinking about gender identity

On 13 February 2014 the online social media networking site Facebook introduced 50+ 'custom gender' descriptors as profile options. For many of the site's then (approximately) 1.3 billion non-trans (or cisgendered) users, this addition was perhaps ignored or overlooked, but enabled others to self-identify in a more nuanced way (Shapiro, 2015). This, together with *Time* magazine's May 2014 front cover headline – 'the transgender tipping point' – along with subsequent mainstream coverage of trans identities marked much greater visibility, though not necessarily a commensurate level of understanding and acceptance. Given general 'familiarity' but also, often unexpressed anxiety and lack of knowledge, terminology seems like a good starting point. Although all language changes over time, for the purposes of clarity here are some key terms which are currently in use:

- **Intersex, or diversity of sex development (DSD)** refers to people who are born with reproductive, chromosomal and/or anatomy that does not appear to fit with typical definitions of male/female.

- **Trans, or transgender** refers to people who do not identify with the gender assigned to them at birth – 'outing' someone's trans identity who does not want it revealed is illegal in the UK and some other countries. It is often used as an umbrella term which includes people who have undergone physical and social transition as well as those who have not.

- **Cis, cisgender or non-trans** refers to people who do identify with the gender assigned to them at birth.

- **Non-binary** refers to people whose identity falls outside the binary male/female and is an umbrella term to include those who might describe themselves as being beyond or outside any gender (such as agender) or whose identity shifts (gender fluid).

Task 11.1

How might autistic and gender-questioning young people be feeling about your lessons? What opportunities and/ or risks might they anticipate? Make lists in pairs (*both* make notes!).

Share your list with a different partner, then share the key points arising with the wider group.

This focus on the (trainee teachers') imagined anxieties of pupils coming to their lessons deliberately brings the needs of the pupils to the forefront of our thinking and should highlight the importance and potential benefits of pre-planning. How might a pupil feel about having a particular characteristic inadvertently highlighted in front of their peers during such routines as taking the register and what impact could this have on their readiness to participate and learn?

A brief reminder is timely here, to highlight pertinent aspects of the (UK) teaching standards, including for example, the establishment of a safe and stimulating environment rooted in mutual respect, and adapting teaching to meet the strengths and needs of all pupils', including a requirement to have a clear understanding of the needs of all pupils and (part two) treating pupils with dignity. Given all this, the question quickly moves to that of classroom practice.

So, how might you shape or adapt your teaching to meet the needs of these pupils (visible to you or not) in ways that might also be beneficial for all? Here are some points for practice, adapted from a list produced by Gendered Intelligence (2017), a trans-led community interest company (CIC) which works specifically with and for young trans and non-binary young people:

- Use gender neutral language until you know someone's choices.

- Learn someone's preferred name and use it, including their pronoun.

- Avoid arbitrary gendered divisions (e.g. 'boys on the left').

- Be mindful of your own gendered expectations and avoid reinforcing gender stereotypes (e.g. boys play football, girls do ballet).

- Challenge and stop HBT (homophobic, biphobic and transphobic) related bullying, including comments or 'jokes'.

- Challenge and stop inappropriate questioning about anatomy.

- Champion each individual pupil's identity, however they may 'present', refraining from making judgements about how well they may or may not appear to 'fit'.

Task 11.2

Working with different partners, make a list of gender neutral terms that you could bring to your teacher language (e.g. pupil; they/their/them – perhaps not so unusual in everyday life – 'someone left *their* bag' on the bus, for example).

Might your pupil groupings (pairs, small group and whole class) need to account for diverse needs as well as being positive and inclusive?

At what points might you as a teacher seem to be governed by a gender binary and, anticipating this, how could you make your practice both principled and flexible to accommodate the needs of all pupils? For example you could cast anyone (gender neutral) to read and/or 'represent' (rather than '*be*') any part in a script.

Share each of these, either one step at a time, or at the end, always remaining solution-focused on 'reasonable adjustments' (as would be the case in an adult employment situation, making the link with life outside and beyond the school gates).

Following the principle that autistic and trans people are likely to be present amongst any cohort of trainee teachers, this next section provides a potential route to bringing voices from the trans and non-binary community directly into the room without placing any individual's personal identity under unwarranted additional scrutiny. The following extracts are drawn from published sources, in order to provide shared points of reference, which offer the perspective of authentic, autobiographical lived experience. It may be worth mentioning that discussions can be conducted in a professional register by imagining the people whose lived experiences are being quoted to be present participants in the room. All this should help trainees to speculate on how teachers might better meet their needs, both as subject teachers and/or as form tutors. The texts also provide touchstones for further reading.

> For the majority of us, when we are born we are cherished by our parents and families. We spend those first few formative years being unconditionally accepted. It is often not until school that we find our first experience of non-acceptance. Here is where we forge friendships and form our social skills, learning to find our level in life, which will go on to either help or hinder us during our time on earth. I most certainly wasn't accepted by everyone during my schooling. Seen as effeminate and attention-seeking, I was pretty much doomed during my time in the tough Barnsley schools I attended. At home though, I felt warmth and love, away from the outside world's preconceptions and judgements... My parents believed in their heart of hearts that if their only child was happy creating their own radio shows in their bedroom, who were they to argue? It was the escapism I needed to get away from the gender dysphoria, along with the continuing bullying and beatings I got at school. (Stephanie Hirst: Burns, 2018, p.346)

School rules and uniforms

'Elementary school students wear uniforms,' the teacher said. To be honest, those things were hideous and I'm positive that most cis kids hated them too, but the nature of my problem was different from theirs. At that time, at around the age of 7, I mostly refused to wear clothes that made me look like a girl and my mom would generally buy me things that I liked. Lucky me! Sadly school regulations couldn't care less about the possibility of some kid questioning the nature of his existence because of the uniforms. I'd been made to wear feminine clothes before that and almost every time I had tantrums about it. But this time, I realised that I would have to wear that thing almost every day for years to come. It felt like being forced into a role that I just couldn't accept. It's hard to describe the feeling when I saw myself in the mirror in the changing room of that shop... Trapped would be a good word. Not trapped in my own body, no. But trapped in the image other people have about me and in the way they treat me just because of a certain body part. 'Where is your uniform?' It's stained. It's being washed. I couldn't find it. It makes my skin itch. I lost it. Insert another random lie here. Actually I had it on every time I left home in the morning, but I made sure to leave early enough so I'd have enough time to hide it in the basement of the building. I knew that everyone around me was making a mistake, but I didn't know yet how to prove it to them. However, I had no intention of feeling horrible every day, not if I could do something about it. (Sasha, Serbia: Mental Health Foundation Scotland, 2018, p.55)

In family, in school and public environments I have always been incorrectly understood. It was enough for the obstetrician to say 'it's a boy!' for my whole life to be predetermined and defined... During my first years of life I always tended to relate more with girls than with boys, as I didn't correspond to the typical stereotype of that age, so I was a laughing stock, a target for discrimination and isolation...I was always put aside in physical education classes, always with the girls...I did not feel integrated in games and activities. The boys were violent with me and I would observe their bad behaviour and wonder how stupid, immature and insensitive they were. I experienced horrible moments of bullying from my family and at school. I am a world of things besides being transgender...I am intelligent, fun, a fighter. I have the talent to cook, make others laugh, give advice, I'm original, cute (some say so), loyal, nice and brave. I never thought I could be this many things at the same time. The human being is so complex. (Andre, Portugal: Mental Health Foundation Scotland, 2018, p.113)

When I was around 14 my school was organising a camping trip and the teacher told me that I wasn't allowed to be in a tent with my exclusively female friends. At the time I didn't know why it bothered me so much. It seemed that I should have just accepted it.

All the other boys who were friends with girls just did. But I was angry. I wanted to scream in the teacher's face and I didn't know why and that confusion made me even angrier. 'Isn't this bullshit?' I whispered to one of my friends. Her look of surprise made me deeply uncomfortable. 'It's not bullshit,' she replied, 'Of course boys and girls have to sleep in different tents. Girls don't want to sleep in a tent with a boy.' That was reasonable wasn't it? So why was I so indignant? 'It's not like we will be in different camp sites or anything; we'll spend most of the trip together anyway. It's just where you'll be sleeping,' she added, seeing my discomfort. But that wasn't the problem was it? It didn't matter how much of the time I spent with my friends because I was the only one of us that didn't get to sleep in the tent with the rest. I was being singled out and treated differently. It was unfair. But why did none of the other boys seem to mind it? About a year after this I realised that the problem was that I am transgender. The camping trip stands out to me as the first time my assigned gender distinctly interfered with what I wanted and how I felt. (Anonymous, Scotland: Mental Health Foundation Scotland, 2018, p.23)

Allowing other people to dictate who we are will only cause us to resent them, and we might even end up angry with ourselves for allowing it all to happen. We might not be able to change our sexual orientation but this is only one aspect of our lives, it does not have to completely rule the rest of our lives... Accepting how we feel isn't always easy and, for some, feeling trapped in a body that yells the opposite to what we feel, and what is expected of us, and so on, can be just too difficult. I have known young people commit suicide rather than live their lives with the confusion and pain of transgender issues. Before you judge us, try to see things from our perspective. If you cannot, then at least accept that we exist and we need your support. It is so much easier to cope with our load when we feel understood. Just because we are individuals on the autistic spectrum, we are not immune from transgender issues. If anything, because we are monotropic, we may well be completely consumed by our transgender feelings and quite obsessive about our cross-gender identity. (Wenn Lawson: Lawson, 2005, p.88)

Task 11.3

Organise yourselves into small-sized 'reading groups' and allocate one of the above extracts per group.

Negotiate a reader to voice the extract to the rest of the group. Consider the lived experience of this person and discuss, as a group, how, as both a subject teacher and/or a form tutor, you might best meet their needs.

Task 11.4

In pairs or small groups, do a 'forensically detailed' review of particular moments in school that you have experienced (either as teacher or observer), which you feel could be improved in relation to meeting the needs of individual autistic and trans pupils.

Gather the key points, practices and principles going forward, and reflect on aspects of teacher thinking, planning and practice.

Key points to bear in mind:

- Autistic, trans and non-binary people do not see themselves as being 'a problem' or 'difficult' unless they are referred to and positioned in this way.

- It is a teacher's professional responsibility to find ways to meet the needs of all pupils.

- This is usually best done by finding out about the needs of individual pupils — there is just as much diversity amongst the autistic, trans and non-binary community as there is in the population at large.

- Expect, plan and teach on the basis that autistic and trans young people are present in all your classes, regardless of whether they are visible and/or identified to you or not.

Further reading

Bouman, W.P. and Arcelus, J. (eds) (2018) *The Transgender Handbook: A Guide for Transgender People, Their Families and Professionals*. New York: Nova Science.

Bornstein, K. (1998) *My Gender Workbook*. New York: Routledge.

Brittain, J. (2015) *Rotterdam*. London/New York: Bloomsbury Methuen Drama.

Henry, D. (2017) *Trans Voices: Becoming Who You Are*. London: Jessica Kingsley Publishers.

Iantaffi, A. and Barker, M.-J. (2018) *How to Understand Your Gender*. London: Jessica Kingsley Publishers.

Lev, A. (2009) *Transgender Emergence: Therapeutic Guidelines for Working with Gender-Variant People and Their Families*. New York/Abingdon: Routledge.

Stryker, S. (2017) *Transgender History: The Roots of Today's Revolution* (2nd edn). New York: Seal Press.

Russo, M. (2016) *If I Was Your Girl*. London:Usborne.

Additional resources

www.mermaidsuk.org.uk/resources-for-professionals.html
There are links from this page to other organisations and resources relevant for all professionals who work with children and young people.

www.schools-out.org.uk/?page_id=156
There are links from this page to material that is particularly focused in and around UK schools.

www.allabouttrans.org.uk/about/
This is the website of an organisation that works with the media to inform their coverage and representation of trans people. A useful place to look to think about attitudes and opinions which circulate in the wider public media coverage of trans folk.

http://libguides.bishopg.ac.uk/c.php?g=164363&p=1079588
A library guide with children's literature list including diverse family books.

References

Bouman, W.P. and Arcelus, J. (2018) *The Transgender Handbook: A Guide for Transgender People, Their Families and Professionals*. New York: Nova Science.

Burns, C. (ed.) (2018) *Trans Britain: Our Journey from the Shadows*. Unbound.

De Vries, A.L., Noens, I.L., Cohen-Kettenis, P.T., van Berckelaer-Onnes, I.A. and Doreleijers, T.A. (2010) Autism spectrum disorders in gender dysphoric children and adolescents. *Journal of Autism and Developmental Disorders 40*, 8, 930–936.

Gendered Intelligence (2017) *Good Practice When Working With Young Trans People*. Work in Education-Good Practice, v1, March 2017. Accessed on 20/12/2018 at http://cdn0.genderedintelligence.co.uk/2017/11/13/15-58-57-Working%20 with%20young%20trans%20people.pdf

Lawson, W. (2005) *Sex, Sexuality and the Autism Spectrum*. London: Jessica Kingsley Publishers.

Mental Health Foundation Scotland (2018) *I Am: Stories from Transgender and Non-binary People across the World*. Glasgow: Mental Health Foundation. www. nationaltheatrescotland.com/wp-content/uploads/2018/06/I-AM_ebook.pdf

Shapiro, E. (2015) *Gender Circuits: Bodies and Identities in a Technological Age*. Abingdon: Routledge.

Chapter Twelve

CHILD NEGLECT OR AUTISM?

How Do You Differentiate?

Sarah Howe

The core objective of this chapter is to develop practitioners' understanding of potential signs of both child neglect and autism and to consider ways to distinguish between them. With the use of case studies and suggested reflection tasks, it will consider 'if', 'when' and 'how', both sets of circumstances could potentially interrelate.

To achieve this objective, practitioners will require:

- knowledge and understanding of the legislative framework for safeguarding and protecting children

- an appreciation that children's welfare is a shared responsibility; this includes a collective obligation to identify concerns, share evidence and act upon this

- awareness of risks and indicators of neglect, alongside the magnitude of its impact on children's lives and development

- sensitive understanding of the diverse behaviours and presentations associated with autism

- knowledge that poor parental behaviours/capacity and environmental factors can result in child neglect

- awareness of the value of active and meaningful communication with all stakeholders, including other professionals and carers.

All children have the right to be safe and protected

This chapter serves to support practitioners to meet their personal and professional responsibilities and duties to safeguard and protect all children while understanding the distinct challenges that autism can bring to that process. It is essential that practitioners have the knowledge and skills to ensure a child's rights are observed and to act in this child's best interests. As a bare minimum, all practitioners should attend appropriate training and professional development and have the confidence to ask questions. Crucially, a setting's policy and procedures require understanding and adherence. When safeguarding thresholds are reached, this may result in a referral to a Local Safeguarding Children Board (LSCB). To enable the requisite safeguarding knowledge and understanding in this complex area, active engagement with numerous sources, especially current Department for Education legislation, is required. All key current documents are located on the Government website at the safeguarding page.[1]

Neglect happens

Safeguarding is 'everyone's responsibility' (DfE, 2018a, p.5). When considering maltreatment, we should all embrace the attitude of 'it could happen here' (DfE, 2018a, p.8) and 'I need to be confident and competent to deal with signs, indicators and disclosures'. Child neglect is a serious and complex subject matter, which requires

---

1   www.gov.uk/topic/schools-colleges-childrens-services/safeguarding-children/latest

judgement. When unidentified or ignored, it has the potential to 'poison childhood and permanently damage life chances', and, sadly, result in fatality (Ventress, 2018, p.72). Neglect can be assessed across a spectrum of levels of concern and is a form of significant harm.

This complexity is reflected in the growth of safeguarding guidance presented to practitioners. Burton (2018) suggests that as a nation, despite previous efforts, we are still struggling with areas of the safeguarding agenda (p.221). However, it is both a statutory obligation and our moral duty, as humans, to understand this subject and act upon any concerns. One alarming statistic is that nearly one in ten children has experienced some form of neglect (Radford *et al.*, 2011, p.14). Neglect happens and is on the increase; between 2016 and 2017, the most common welfare concern reported to the NSPCC's helpline related to neglect. This equated to 19,448 telephone contacts during this one-year period (Bentley *et al.*, 2017, p.39). In England, neglect is the most common reason cited for a child being placed in the child protection system (Bentley *et al.*, 2017, p.56). Despite our responsibilities to safeguard children, there is a perceived time and resource pressure within the Social Care system (Community Care, 2012).

Neglect is complex and often moves beyond obvious physical signs such as inappropriate clothing and poor hygiene. It can be a consequence of poor parental supervision/capacity and living conditions, which can ultimately compromise a child's safety. We know that indicators of neglect are not always experienced in isolation; the indicators often occur alongside undetected abuse (physical, emotional and/or sexual). This is the unfortunate outcome of many Serious Case Reviews (SCRs); 60 per cent of the 139 reviews undertaken in England between 2009 and 2011 found neglect to be a significant factor (Brandon *et al.*, 2013, p.7).

There is a spectrum of urgency; neglect can occur at different frequency and severity. The crux is getting the 'right help at the right time to address risks and prevent issues escalating' (DfE, 2016, p.9). Some carers' disregard for children's welfare needs can start suddenly, especially because of rapid changes to parenting capacity, such as mental health issues, or family composition. A challenge for practitioners, after considering carefully all of the facts and presentations, is making the correct judgement on the degree of severity, when action is required and what action is in the best interests of the child. Intentional neglect is a criminal offence. As Brandon *et al.* (2014) and the DfE (2018a) advocate, support, often in the form of 'Early Help', needs to be offered to the child and families at all stages of concern. If practitioners are in any doubt about a child's welfare, concerns must be shared with appropriate professionals and bodies. If the child is experiencing significant harm, or, in the opinion of the practitioner, likely to experience significant harm, an immediate referral to local authority children's social care is needed.

Task 12.1

The DfE (2018a, p.15) defines neglect as:

The persistent failure to meet a child's basic physical and/or psychological needs, likely to result in the serious impairment of the child's health or development. Neglect may occur during pregnancy, for example, as a result of maternal substance abuse. Once a child is born, neglect may involve a parent or carer failing to: provide adequate food, clothing and shelter (including exclusion from home or abandonment); protect a child from physical and emotional harm or danger; ensure adequate supervision (including the use of inadequate care-givers); or ensure access to appropriate medical care or treatment. It may also include neglect of, or unresponsiveness to, a child's basic emotional needs.

The DfE's definition of child neglect has limitations. In pairs, identify and discuss any areas of ambiguity.

- Which terms and phrases require further clarity?

- Are SEND adequately represented within this definition?

- Could a definition ever capture all aspects of neglect?

Neglect can be 'at least' as damaging as other forms of abuse (Brandon *et al.*, 2014, p.13). This persistent failure to meet basic physical and psychological needs can damage a child's 'typical' development trajectory and have enduring impact. This could include delayed development in aspects of physical, neurobiological and language and communication development, as well as mental health, social functioning and coping mechanism difficulties. This is especially so within the early years of child development (Brandon *et al.*, 2014; Ventress, 2018). Child neglect can significantly jeopardise development throughout childhood and adolescence. This, in turn, can influence child functioning and attributes which may be evident in adulthood, for example, self-confidence, resilience and impulsive behaviour.

Autistic children are vulnerable

Autistic children are vulnerable; they are classified as 'disabled' and as such they are 'significantly' more likely to experience neglect or abuse than their non-disabled peers (Stalker and McArthur, 2012, p.24). This vulnerability is aggravated by autistic deficits in social communication and social interaction, as discussed in Chapter One.

Although no two children with autism have identical presentations and behaviours, all autistic children are vulnerable. Limited training on autism in schools (APPGA, 2017) will impact on practitioners' understanding of autism and this may affect their ability to identify and differentiate the signs of neglect. For example, autistic children show abnormal social emotional responses, which can result in limited engagement in back-and-forth conversations. This means that practitioners are challenged to accurately gauge children's life stories and emotions. Fundamentally, autism calls for alternative means of evidence gathering.

Practitioners must be mindful that the autistic child's family are also considered vulnerable. They may be challenged by their child's or sister's/brother's disability. These difficulties include understanding a child's disability and feeling stigmatised by, and isolated from, all those around them (Falk, Norris and Quinn, 2014). Kuusikko-Gauffin *et al.*'s (2013) social anxiety study in carers of children with autism suggests a child's disability can also have an impact on their carer's mental health and well-being. This research concluded that a carer's well-being 'may contribute greatly' to an autistic child's emotional development (p.521). This links to Falk *et al.* (2014)'s claim that existing literature demonstrates that 'the parents of children with autism report *more* mental health problems than the parents of children in other clinical and/or non-clinical groups' (p.3185). For this reason, practitioners must appreciate that having an autistic child in a family can, sometimes, heighten other common contemporary challenges experienced by families. This is aggravated further when the family are also experiencing the impact of poverty.

Autistic behaviours may be mistaken for, or may mask, neglect

Task 12.2

Consider the autism diagnostic descriptors from DSM-5 (American Psychiatric Association, 2013) in the table below. How can autistic presentation create a challenge to professionals alert for potential neglect? What misunderstandings may occur when differentiating between autistic traits and signs and indicators of neglect?

A: Persistent deficits in social communication and social interaction	Manifestation examples	Potential safeguarding and child protection challenges
Deficits in social-emotional reciprocity	Limited conversation and social interactions; Reduced expression of emotions	
Deficits in non-verbal communicative behavior used for social interactions	Poor verbal and non-verbal communication; Lack of facial expression	
Deficits in developing, maintaining, and understanding relationships	Difficulty adjusting behavior according to the context; Difficulty in making and maintaining friendships; absence of interest in peers	
B: Restricted and repetitive patterns of behavior, interests, or activities	**Manifestation examples**	**Potential safeguarding and child protection challenges**
Stereotyped or repetitive motor movements, use of objects, or speech	Use of idiosyncratic phrases; Repetition of another's words	
Insistence on sameness, inflexible adherence to routines, or ritualised patterns of verbal or nonverbal behavior	Extreme distress when experiencing changes to routine; The establishment of rituals; Requires the same food every day	

Highly restricted, fixated interests that are abnormal in intensity or focus	Strong attachment to or preoccupation with unusual things; Fixated, potentially obsessional interest
Sensory processing differences Hyper-or hyperactivity to sensory input or unusual interests in sensory aspects of the environment	Heightened sensitivity to or indifferent to pain; Adverse responses to specific sounds, smells or textures; Excessive smelling and touching; Visual fascination with lights and movement

The remainder of this chapter comprises three case studies and reflective tasks that have been designed to promote thought, discussion and debate. They provide the opportunity to consider the key signs and indicators of neglect, including circumstances in which autistic behaviours and presentations may be misinterpreted. There is also the opportunity to contemplate circumstances in which seeming autism presentations and behaviours may mask potential neglect. The three key discussion themes are those of self-care, sleep, and health, specifically that of dental health.

Key discussion theme one: self-care

Neglect is the failure to meet a child's physical needs. This may be manifested in inadequate or inappropriate clothing (clothing that is not appropriate for the weather or time of year; lack of adherence to school uniform requirements). The child's hair may be unbrushed or unclean, and the child may appear dirty or may smell.

The autistic child's lens

The autistic child may be less motivated by societal norms (fitting in with the dress code of peers), and more by sensory issues. Clothing may be chosen for comfort, and the same items worn repeatedly. Some autistic people find their own odours reassuring, and – conversely – may find the smell of washing powders and conditioners repellent (Bogdashina, 2016). Similarly, hair may preferably be washed without use of shampoo, and there may be reluctance generally to use soap or shower gel.

Many autistic children, regardless of cognitive or functional level, find interoception messages difficult to interpret. This may result in an inability to know when they are hungry or thirsty, or to recognise the need to empty bladder or bowels (Bogdashina, 2016). Incontinence is relatively prevalent in autism, with a corresponding perceived social stigma of being 'smelly' or 'dirty'.

Case Study 1: 'Ben'

Here are two reflective observations – Ben's physical presentation is considered from the teacher's and mother's lenses.

The teacher's lens:

Ben is new to the school this year and is in Year 4. His shirt is a dirty grey, his trousers are not regulation uniform and his shoes are coming apart. His hair is lank and in desperate need of a cut. His faded lunchbox has a broken hinge and the contents are dull and unimaginative; they are always the same.

At the end of the school day Ben is collected by a tired-looking woman who is his mother. They do not exchange a greeting or share a hug. They move off towards the school gate at the same time, and in the same direction, but separate – running parallel like railway tracks.

Ben seldom interacts with other children and avoids physical contact. If another child accidentally brushes up

---

against him, he winces. He seldom runs, laughs or skips and looks more like an old man than a child.

The mother's lens:

Ben's shirt is a dirty grey because he hates wearing new ones. Anything new itches and irritates, and it was only when this shirt – which was purchased last week – had been washed and re-washed to a limp, exhausted, rag-like texture that it was comfortable for him to wear. The same is true of his trousers. Ben hates the feeling of long trousers on his legs and would always prefer to wear shorts (which are not allowed in the school's uniform rules). The three-quarter length trousers are a compromise which the school has so far tolerated. Ben finds all shopping overwhelming. I can buy clothes for him on the internet, but his shoes need to be properly fitted. We only make a trip to buy new shoes – or for the equally loathed haircut – during the holidays when Ben has fewer pressures. His lunch, carried in his old and much-loved lunchbox, has been negotiated between us as being nutritionally balanced but acceptable. It is identical each day to provide him with the security that enables him to eat.

Ben is exhausted at the end of each school day. We always walk home in silence. By the time we get there he has recovered enough to have a glass of milk and a banana while we try to sort out the many confusions and anxieties that the day at school has produced.

Task 12.3

Consider this case study from the lenses of both the teacher and mother.

- What impressions might you have without the mother's explanation?

- As a practitioner, would you remain worried about Ben's welfare?

- Based on all of the information, what would your next steps be?

Key discussion theme two: sleep

Sleep plays a vital role in maintaining health and promoting academic progress and optimal functioning. Recommended sleeping time can vary according to the age of the child. Pre-school children (three- to four-year-olds) require around 11 hours sleep each night in order to function appropriately, with older children requiring between nine and ten hours (NHS, n.d.). When sleep is compromised, it can affect several aspects of the child functioning, for instance, mental health, physical activity and ability to learn and concentrate. Long-term sleep deficiency can manifest itself in low energy levels and hyperactivity. Additionally, inadequate sleep can lead to an imbalance in hormone levels, which can influence growth. Practitioners should be mindful that a deficit in sleep can also have significant impact on the daily functioning of others in the household; this includes both carers and siblings.

Environmental factors may influence a child's quality of sleep, for example, household conditions such as: ventilation, sound insulation, number of bedrooms in the household and room temperature. For some families, meeting such conditions can present a challenge, particularly for those experiencing poverty.

The autistic child's lens

It is relatively common for autistic children to have difficulties initiating and maintaining adequate sleep. Some suggest that sleep problems with autistic children are both 'under-recognised' and 'undertreated' (Tilford *et al.*, 2015, p.3613). Sensory differences and difficulty in understanding the need to sleep can make it harder for the child to relax and prepare themselves for this. Like their peers, sleep challenges can exacerbate daytime behaviours and functioning. For an autistic child, this can be reflected in increased stereotypical behaviours and social and emotional difficulties (Schoen, Man and Spiro, 2017). Practitioners may find these hard to understand and interpret. Some children lack the ability to social cue – they may not 'read' another's behaviours and make the connection that it is bedtime for all in the household (especially during the months with extended daylight). In addition, some children will require consistent reassurance and robust routines to enable this activity. If these features are compromised, it can upset the usual pattern of sleep and this, ultimately, will affect the child's, and others', sleep quality within the household.

Case Study 2: 'Ravi'

Ravi is 10 years old. He was diagnosed with autism at the age of four and at the same time was judged to have an IQ of 136. He has difficulty both falling asleep and staying asleep. He has a bed-time routine that includes no screen-time, a bath, a warm drink, his father reading him a story, music and a nightlight. His parents recently introduced a 'Thoughts Book' where he can record questions, concerns and ideas to be discussed during the daytime to reduce anxiety at night. Despite these, Ravi is awake frequently during the night, needing to seek reassurance and to have his repeated questions answered.

Task 12.4

Consider some of the additional challenges that some households face when an autistic child does not fall asleep easily or is prone to awaking several times during the night.

- How will this impact on both the child and other household members?

- When bedrooms are shared, what are some potential challenges for both the autistic child and their siblings?

- What home improvements might help? Can these be limited by financial hardship?

Key discussion theme three: dental health

Dental health concerns are on the rise in England; dental pain is the most common cause of hospitalisation in five- to nine-year-old children (PHE, 2017). In order to remove and treat infected carious teeth, some children will require general anaesthesia, which comes with risks of complication. There is some concern about there being no threshold number of carious teeth to constitute dental health neglect, which can result in dentists and dental care professionals' failure to report neglect (Bhatia *et al.*, 2013, p.229). Consequently, professional judgement is required and relied upon. Carers can neglect a child's oral health needs by not attending dental appointments, failing to promote the regular brushing of their child's teeth and by providing too many foods and drinks comprising high sugar content. There may be a 'failure or delay in seeking treatment for significant dental caries or trauma' or carers may allow 'the child's oral health to deteriorate avoidably' (Bhatia *et al.*, 2013, p.237). This dental neglect and pain will impact on many aspects of their childs' daily life such as their eating activity, communication, quality of sleep, social activity and concentration levels. Most poor dental health is avoidable and can be supported by regular brushing with a fluoride toothpaste, regular monitoring visits at a dentist surgery and a healthy diet.

The autistic child's lens

Autistic children are reliant on their carers to maintain good oral health. However, oral health carries significant challenges for many autistic people (Bossù *et al.*, 2014; Muthu and Prathibha, 2008) and resulting lack of oral care may result in autistic children having increased incidence of dental caries (Jaber, 2011). Autistic children may resist teeth cleaning totally, may only tolerate use of a dry brush or be unable to make the move from 'child' to 'adult' toothpaste.

Parents may be reluctant to insist on teeth brushing as part of a bedtime routine if this is already a challenging time and calmness to aid sleep may be the priority. A consistent routine for teeth brushing may be difficult to implement, and a food-based motivator (for example a lollipop or a sweet) may be used reinforce brushing.

Regular dental check-ups and the management of dental issues may be a further challenge:

> In autistic children a major obstacle arising during dental care treatments is anxiety. A dentist room, with its peculiar environment and equipment, may represent a very fearful stimulus. Some patients react with overt uncooperative behaviour such as crying or physical and verbal aggression in order to avoid the treatments. (Bossù *et al.*, 2014, p.108)

Understanding of autism by dental surgeries can allow for compensatory measures to be put in place. The visit may be prepared for, time waiting minimised and 'dry-run' visits undertaken. The child may be supported to wear headphones and/or listen to recordings of familiar and favourite stories or soundtracks, and some dentists project films or cartoons onto the ceiling of the surgery.

All dentist surgeries should have had training regarding the treating of autistic patients and be able to offer advice on managing surgery visits. In reality, though, levels of care and understanding are uneven across different practices.

Case Study 3: 'Sarah'

Sarah is four years old. She is autistic and currently is pre-verbal.

In Nursery today, Sarah is drooling and pushing away both food and drink. You are concerned that Sarah may be experiencing dental pain. Her mother mentioned nothing about this when she brought her into nursery today.

You immediately phone home in order to express your concern about possible toothache. Sarah's mother agrees and comments that both she and her partner have thought the same since Friday (three days ago). You ask if they have checked her mouth. The mother informs you that Sarah absolutely refuses to let anyone check (or clean) her teeth; attempts to do this result in Sarah getting extremely distressed and it can then take some time for her to calm down.

Sarah's mother also comments that her daughter's sleep and eating are both compromised. When asked about making a dental appointment, she says that their dentist 'doesn't know anything about autism' and that at the previous visit he couldn't even get Sarah to open her mouth. She feels that visiting the surgery is therefore pointless and that, should things not improve by the end of the week, she might be able to ask her GP for a referral to the hospital where she has heard from another mother that there is a more autism aware service.

Task 12.5

Consider this case study from the lenses of the child, parent and childcare setting.

- Does this constitute neglect?

- How would you respond to this information?

Conclusion

With some children, it is more difficult to identify indicators of neglect. For example, autistic children may have communication differences or challenges, may misunderstand others' intentions and have presentations and behaviours that differ to their peers (yet work for them). This chapter has explored some examples, but practitioners should remain alert to the many different manifestations of autism. They will require confidence to challenge others constructively to ensure they fulfil their professional duties and to meet the needs and interests of these vulnerable children. Practitioners also need to be mindful that some carers' choices about childcare methods may differ from theirs but remain valid. However, they should also be aware of the wider vulnerability of parents and carers who may be struggling to meet the needs of their autistic children with little or no support. Always, if welfare is deemed to be compromised, statutory procedures must be followed. The need to share information and work with some 'more knowledgeable' professionals and bodies is critical if 'grey areas' are identified. This supports the principle of 'Working Together to Safeguard Children' (DfE, 2018b).

It is hard to construct the communication and sensory world of autism. This chapter has captured a few, of many, instances where autistic behaviour may indicate neglect but actually transpire, instead, to be a feature of autism. However, it has equally sought to highlight that the presence of autism should never be an excuse for ignoring signs of potential neglect. Practitioners should think carefully before adopting the 'let's wait and see' approach or categorising certain behaviours, which could be presentations of neglect, as 'it's the autism'. Instead, they should exercise a growth mindset, adhere to safeguarding and child protection policy and procedures, and exercise professional curiosity. The following box lists seven key points for the practitioner to consider. The safeguarding process requires sensitivity, pro-activity, confidence and motivation.

Negotiate, with understanding, the legislative documentation provided to safeguard children. Understand your central role in ensuring all children are safe and free from harm. Everyone has an essential role in identifying and assessing concerns, sharing information and acting upon this.

Engage in meaningful dialogue and assessment with your designated safeguarding lead (DSL), SENCo, other key professionals and with parents. Share information and act on this appropriately. This may meet the threshold for an immediate referral to a local safeguarding board.

Gauge the individual developmental and learning needs of the child through professional curiosity. In most instances, this requires communication with the child and their carers/carers. Understand any family and environmental barriers and parental capacity needs. Early Help should be utilised as soon as a problem emerges. If the threshold for Early Help is not met, practitioners should work with their

DSL to signpost parents/carers to appropriate support and services.

Learn the signs and indicators of neglect. How can these be missed, misunderstood or ignored? Be an advocate for every child in your care.

Educate yourself on all aspects of autism. How can autism influence a child's social communication and behaviours? Lack of understanding may result in a misinterpretation of neglect or overlooking the rights and welfare needs of an autistic child.

Communicate sensitively and in a timely way with the child, family and other professionals. As the focus is on the child, this communication may take a range of forms, dependent on the child's preferred communication method. Close observations and monitoring will be an outcome of initial concerns. If the child is at risk of significant harm, it is fundamental that policy and procedures are followed. No sole professional can have a full and true picture of that child's needs and life – concerns need to be discussed.

Translate this knowledge and understanding of neglect, including possible indicators, into confident practice. Know how to intervene and challenge others – the child's welfare must be at the heart of all actions taken.

References

APPGA (All Party Parliamentary Group on Autism) (2017) Autism and Education in England 2–17. A report by the All Party Parliamentary Group on Autism on how the education system in England works for children and young people on the autism spectrum. Accessed on 10/10/2018 at www.autism.org.uk/get-involved/campaign/appga/highlights.aspx

American Psychiatric Association (2013) *Diagnostic and Statistical Manual of Mental Disorders* (5th edn). Washington, DC: APA.

Bentley, H., O'Hagan, O., Brown, A., Vasco, N. *et al.* (2017) *How Safe Are Our Children? The Most Comprehensive Overview of Child Protection in the UK 2017.* London: NSPCC.

Bhatia, S., Maguire, S., Chadwick, B., Hunter, L. *et al.* (2013) Characteristics of child dental neglect: A systematic review. *Journal of Dentistry 42*, 229–239.

Bogdashina, O. (2016) *Sensory Perceptual Issues in Autism and Asperger Syndrome* (2nd edn). London: Jessica Kingsley Publishers.

Bossù, M., Corridore, D., D'Errico, A., Ladniak, B., Ottolenghi, L. and Polimeni, A. (2014) Education and dentistry: Advanced synergy in the dental treatment of children with autism; a pilot clinical trial. *Senses and Sciences 1*, 3, 107–111.

Brandon, M., Bailey, S., Belderson, P. and Larsson, B. (2013) *Neglect and Serious Case Reviews. A report from the University of East Anglia commissioned by NSPCC.* Accessed on 03/12/2018 at https://learning.nspcc.org.uk/media/1053/neglect-serious-case-reviews-report.pdf

Brandon, M., Glaser, D., Maguire, S., McCrory, E., Lushey, C. and Ward, H. (2014) *Missed Opportunities: Indicators of Neglect – What is Ignored, Why, and What Can Be Done?* Research report. Accessed on 10/10/2018 at www.cwrc.ac.uk/documents/RR404_-_Indicators_of_neglect_missed_opportunities.pdf

Burton, S. (2018) 'Conclusion.' In S. Burton and J. Reid (eds) *Safeguarding and Protecting Children in the Early Years* (2nd edn). Abingdon: Routledge.

Community Care (2012) Social Workers Unlikely to Act Quickly on Neglect Cases. Accessed on 09/10/2018 at www.communitycare.co.uk/2012/09/26/social-workers-unlikely-to-act-quickly-on-neglect-cases-2

Department for Education (2016) *Keeping Children Safe in Education: Statutory Guidance for Schools and Colleges.* Accessed on 08/10/2018 at www.gov.uk/government/publications/keeping-children-safe-in-education--2

Department for Education (2018a) *Keeping Children Safe in Education: Statutory guidance for schools and colleges.* Accessed on 23/01/2019 at https://assets.publishing.service.gov.uk/government/uploads/system/uploads/attachment_data/file/741314/Keeping_Children_Safe_in_Education__3_September_2018_14.09.18.pdf

Department for Education (2018b) *Working Together to Safeguard Children: A Guide to Inter-Agency Working to Safeguard and Promote the Welfare of Children.* Accessed on 10/10/2018 at https://assets.publishing.service.gov.uk/government/uploads/system/uploads/attachment_data/file/722305/Working_Together_to_Safeguard_Children_-_Guide.pdf

Falk, N., Norris, K. and Quinn, M. (2014) The factors predicting stress, anxiety and depression in the carers of children with autism. *Journal of Autism and Developmental Disorders 44*, 3185–3203.

Jaber, M.A. (2011) Dental caries experience, oral health status and treatment needs of dental patients with autism. *Journal of Applied Oral Science 19*, 3, 212–217.

Kuusikko-Gauffin, S., Pollock-Wurman, R., Mattila, M., Jussila, K. *et al.* (2013) Social anxiety in carers of high-functioning children with autism and Asperger Syndrome. *Journal of Autism and Developmental Disorder 43*, 521–529.

Muthu, M. and Prathibha, K. (2008) Management of a child with autism and severe bruxism: A case report. *Journal of Indian Society of Pedodontics and Preventive Dentistry 26*, 2, 82. Accessed on 10/10/2018 at http://link.galegroup.com/apps/doc/A181066631/AONE?u=bgc&sid=AONE&xid=d1e5a805

NHS (National Health Service) (n.d.) Sleep and Tiredness. Accessed on 10/10/2018 at www.nhs.uk/live-well/sleep-and-tiredness/how-much-sleep-do-kids-need

PHE (Public Health England) (2017) *Guidance – Health Matters: Child Dental Health.* Accessed on 10/10/2018 at www.gov.uk/government/publications/health-matters-child-dental-health/health-matters-child-dental-health

Radford, L., Corral, S., Bradley, C., Fisher, H. *et al.* (2011) *Child Abuse and Neglect in the UK Today.* London: NSPCC.

Schoen, S., Man, S. and Spiro, C. (2017) A sleep intervention for Autism Spectrum Disorder: A pilot study. *The Open Journal of Occupational Therapy 5*, 2, Article 3.

Stalker, K. and McArthur, K. (2012) Child abuse, child protection and disabled children: A review of recent research, *Child Abuse Review 21*,1, 24–40.

Tilford, M., Payakachat, N., Kuhlthau, K., Pyne, J. *et al.* (2015) Treatment for sleep problems in children with autism and caregivers spillover effects. *Journal of Autism and Developmental Disorders 45*, 3613–3623.

Ventress, N. (2018) 'Neglect in the Early Years.' In S. Burton and J. Reid (eds) *Safeguarding and Protecting Children in the Early Years* (2nd edn). Abingdon: Routledge.

Chapter Thirteen

'SO, THIS IS WHAT REALLY HAPPENED...'

Using Story to Explore Theory of Mind, Perspectives, Autobiographical Recall and Event Reconstruction with Autistic Pupils

---

Clare Lawrence

As discussed (Chapter One), difficulties with Theory of Mind (ToM) can mean that autistic pupils struggle to see a situation from any but their own perspective. If their behaviour makes sense to them, they may see little reason to explain or modify it. What is more, if what they did was 'right' in their eyes, they may feel justified anger if they are penalised for their actions. Unpicking motives for autistic behaviours can be difficult, particularly in a school environment. Schools tend to have simple, concrete rules: 'No hitting' means just that, and no amount of justification may be allowed to deflect the repercussions for hitting out. Yet no rule is absolute in reality. If a colleague were choking, it is quite likely that any one of us would hit that person (hard) in the back to attempt to dislodge the blockage.

There has been a strong link established between autistic behaviours and ToM difficulties (e.g. Frith, Morton and Leslie, 1991; Jones *et al.*, 2018). Getting to the bottom of reality as it is experienced by the autistic pupil, and therefore unpicking 'what happened' for them, can be a real challenge. One way of approaching the issue is to use story. Story-based approaches such as Social Stories™ (Gray and Garand, 1993) and Comic Strip Conversations (Gray, 1994; 1998) are widely used with autistic children to facilitate social understanding. The structure of a story, and the reduced emotive context of fiction, may be useful tools to help autistic pupils access autobiographical memory and reconstruct scenes, both critical skills for organising and understanding personally experienced events (Hutchins and Prelock, 2018).

What follows is a story, told twice from different viewpoints. These stories are written for one-to-one use with Key Stage 2 pupils with autism but may also be useful in Key Stage 3 and in a classroom context. They are a way of exploring the concepts of different perspectives with autistic pupils, both to explore how they can see another person's point of view, and to increase awareness that other people including teachers and parents do not know what happens unless they explain it. They are taken from *Exploring Theory of Mind with Children on the Autism Spectrum: Two Sides to Every Story* (Lawrence, 2019).

Task 13.1

Divide the group into A and B and give out versions accordingly. When they have read their version, ask B to question A as to what happened, A's motives, A's feelings and so on. A can only answer 'Yes' or 'No'.

Bryn and the pushchair baby (A)

Bryn liked ice-cream.

1. The first ice-cream is thought to have been made in Ancient Persia by pouring grape juice over snow.

2. Ice-cream is stirred as it cools to trap air and give it its creamy texture.

3. The most popular flavours of ice-cream are vanilla and chocolate.

4. Ice-cream made with fruit juice rather than dairy products is called sorbet.

Bryn liked ice-cream because it was cold and felt good in his mouth. He liked ice-cream when the weather was hot, but he also liked it when it was cold. Bryn's mum bought ice-cream all year round and kept it in the freezer for treats.

In the summer the post-office served ice-cream in cones, and Bryn's mum said that Bryn could have one ice-cream from there a week. He still had his other ice-cream at home, but the bought one was really special. Bryn could choose when to have his ice-cream. He tried to save it until the weekend as something to look forward to, but sometimes he couldn't resist. This week Bryn's mum had called in at the post-office on Monday on the way home from school and Bryn had had his ice-cream then. It had been delicious!

Now it was Friday, and Bryn's mum called in at the post-office again. Bryn knew that he couldn't have an ice-cream. He knew the rules. Bryn waited outside the post-office while his mum went in to post a parcel.

Bryn watched two other mums standing talking. One had a big brown dog on a long blue rope lead and a tiny baby asleep in a pram. The baby was wrapped up in a yellow and white striped sheet with its head sticking out. It had its thumb stuck in its mouth and every so often it sucked on its thumb and its eyes moved around behind its closed lids. Bryn guessed that it was dreaming, and he wondered what babies dream about.

The other mum had a slightly older child strapped into a push chair. This baby was wide awake and sitting up. It had a red t-shirt and green trousers with little patterns of leaves on them. It had an ice-cream.

Bryn didn't think the baby knew about ice-cream. Bryn knew that you have to lick all around the ice-cream, and keep turning the cone, otherwise the ice-cream melts and starts to drip. The baby was just sucking at one side of the ice-cream. It had ice-cream all over its face and the rest of the ice-cream was dripping down the cone and onto its red t-shirt and over the baby's hand and onto the baby's green, leaf-patterned trousers. It was making a dreadful mess.

The baby seemed confused by the feeling of cold as the ice-cream melted all over it. It held the ice-cream out towards its mother, but she didn't notice. She was still talking. Someone did notice, though, and that was the dog.

Bryn didn't think this dog was wise at all. If it were it would know that it is very unhygienic for a dog to lick an ice-cream held by a baby. It would know that its tongue is covered in germs and that those germs can be dangerous for humans, particularly new humans who haven't had time to build up their immunity yet.

Bryn watched the dog lick the ice-cream. He watched the baby start to put the ice-cream back to its own mouth. Bryn took the two steps needed and took the ice-cream out of the baby's hand.

Several things happened at once. Bryn's mum came out of the post-office and said, 'Bryn!' quite loudly. The baby gave a great wail. The dog pulled towards Bryn, following the ice-cream, and got the first mother all tangled up. The first mother's tiny baby woke up, took its thumb out of its mouth and gave a hiccupping sob and the second mother grabbed hold of Bryn's arm.

'What the heck do you think you're doing?' she shouted, her face right up to Bryn's. He tried to answer but she kept shaking his arm and he couldn't find the words. Both babies were roaring; Bryn's mum was shouting, 'Leave him alone! Let go of him!' again and again, and the dog started barking and barking and barking.

Bryn's eyes burned.

Bryn's ears buzzed.

Bryn's hands clenched, and his knees locked.

'AAAAAGGGHH!'

Bryn and the pushchair baby (B)

Bryn's mum liked to use the local post-office.

1. Local shops are an important part of the community.

2. Marge, who worked in the shop, had been Bryn's mum's friend since school.

3. Calling at the post-office gave Bryn's mum a chance to chat with local people.

4. In the summer she could buy Bryn an ice-cream, once a week, as a treat.

Bryn's mum wished that she could buy Bryn an ice-cream every time she went to the shop, but the ice-creams were expensive. It was much cheaper to buy a big tub from the supermarket and keep it in the freezer. She had agreed the 'once a week' rule with Bryn, and she knew that it was good for him to have rules...but still, she wished she could buy him his treat every time.

Today she was calling at the post-office to send a present to America. Her sister had moved there over a year ago and now had a little girl of her own. The present was a lift-the-flap book for the niece she had never met. Bryn's mum wished that they lived nearer so that she could see them more often.

Marge had some interesting news about a local meeting. Marge said that there was going to be a meeting at the village hall next week and that Bryn's mum should come along.

Bryn's mum was thinking about the meeting as she left the shop. It was at seven o'clock, so perhaps she might be able to go and to take Bryn with her. He was no trouble and should be happy for an hour or so reading his science book. She looked to see what he was doing now as he waited for her.

To her astonishment she saw Bryn walk up to a baby in a pushchair and steal its ice-cream. She couldn't believe her eyes! 'Bryn!' she called out.

Bryn stood there with the ice-cream in his hand. The baby started crying and Bryn's mum felt terrible. Then the baby's mum got cross and started shouting at Bryn. Bryn's mum wasn't having that. Even if Bryn had taken the ice-cream, that woman had no right to shout at her son, and certainly no right to shake him.

'Leave him alone!' Bryn's mum shouted. 'Let go of him!' The other woman's dog started barking and her baby started screaming too. Still the stupid woman was shaking Bryn by the arm. She had to stop. Bryn wouldn't be able to cope with that.

'Leave him alone, I said', Bryn's mum said, as loudly as she could... but it was too late. Bryn's hands were clenched, and his knees were locked.

'AAAAAGGGHH!'

Task 13.2

The story finishes with a coda, which offers resolution and reassurance. What has Bryn learned from this incident? What have other characters learned? Why does Wise Dog say the things he does?

Coda

Bryn's door swung slowly open. A weight settled itself with a sigh on the foot of his bed.

'I don't understand you.'

Bryn could only hear Wise Dog in these few minutes before he fell asleep. The rest of the time Wise Dog was just the old family mongrel, who answered (when he felt like it) to the name of Max. Wise Dog only seemed to exist in this grey world as Bryn's eyes grew heavy and the light faded away.

'Why didn't you tell her why you took the ice-cream? She thinks you were stealing it and she's really disappointed in you.' Wise Dog shook his great, hairy head slowly from side to side. 'You have to explain to her, Bryn.'

Bryn sighed. 'I tried. I tried to tell her that germs are dangerous for young humans. I tried to tell her about how the immune system takes time to mature, but she wasn't listening. When she's upset, she doesn't listen properly to what I'm saying.'

Wise Dog gave a nod. 'Who does that remind me of? I don't know, you humans are a funny lot! Tell you what, tomorrow, when she has calmed down, you can explain to her properly. She'll listen then.'

'Yes. I'll tell her in the morning. I don't like her thinking I would steal from that baby, but at least I know I did the right thing. I saved it from getting ill, and even if they all think I did a wrong thing, I know that what I did was right.'

Wise Dog was silent for a while, thinking that over. 'Do you know, you're right, young Bryn. There's many people twice your age who don't understand that. What you did was right, and no amount of misunderstanding can take that away from you. Well done. I'm very proud of you.'

Bryn felt happy. If Wise Dog was proud of him, then he must be OK. And tomorrow he would explain to his mum – and then she would be proud of him too.

'Goodnight, Wise Dog.'

'Goodnight, Bryn.'

Boy and dog slept.

Task 13.3

How could you use these stories in a classroom environment? In your groups, design questions to discuss and activities which could be used with your pupils, both autistic and neurotypical.

Here are some examples:

Questions to discuss:

- Why can't Bryn have an ice-cream every time they visit the post-office? There is more than one answer to this question!

- Why doesn't Bryn's mum listen when he tries to explain why he took the ice-cream?

- What evidence can you find in this story that suggests that Bryn's mum may be rather lonely?

- 'There's many people twice your age who don't understand that.' What does Wise Dog mean?

Suggested activities:

1. Bryn likes ice-cream because it is cold, and he likes the feeling of it. Other people dislike ice-cream because they don't like the feeling of cold. How we experience the same thing varies from person to person. To experience this, try the 'temperature experiment': Get three bowls of water, one cold, one hot (but not scalding) and one about body temperature. Put one hand in the cold bowl and one in the hot bowl. Then put both your hands together in the middle bowl. What do you feel? Can you explain what is happening?

2. Try making your own sorbet. You don't need any special equipment and you can experiment with different fruits.

Strawberry sorbet

You will need:

2lbs fresh strawberries
Sugar
Water
Lemon juice

Method:

Stir one cup of sugar into one cup of water.
Simmer for five minutes and allow to cool.
Pour the cooled syrup over the strawberries and blend until smooth.
Strain the mixture through a sieve.
Stir in one teaspoon of lemon juice.
Put in the fridge for at least one hour.
Give the cold mixture a really good stir, then put in freezer for at least four hours.
Scoop out your strawberry sorbet and enjoy!

1. Has there ever been a time when you have been misunderstood and something that you have done has been misinterpreted? Now is your chance to tell your side of the story!

2. Imagine you are Marge from the post-office. What did you see that day? Write a storyboard giving just the facts, but in a clear order.

References

Frith, U., Morton, J. and Leslie, A.M. (1991) The cognitive basis of a biological disorder: Autism. *Trends in Neurosciences 14*, 10, 433–438.

Gray, C. (1994) *Comic Strip Conversations: Illustrated Interactions that Teach Conversation Skills to Students with Autism and Related Disorders.* Arlington, TX: Future Horizons.

Gray, C.A. (1998) 'Social Stories™ and Comic Strip Conversations with Students with Asperger Syndrome and High-Functioning Autism.' In E. Schopler, G.B. Mesibov and L. Kunce (eds) *Asperger Syndrome or High-Functioning Autism?* Boston, MA: Springer.

Gray, C.A. and Garand, J.D. (1993) Social stories™: Improving responses of students with autism with accurate social information. *Focus on Autistic Behavior 8,* 1, 1–10.

Hutchins, T.L. and Prelock, P.A. (2018) Using story-based interventions to improve episodic memory in autism spectrum disorder. *Seminars in Speech and Language 39,* 2, 125–143.

Jones, C.R., Simonoff, E., Baird, G., Pickles, A. *et al.* (2018) The association between theory of mind, executive function, and the symptoms of autism spectrum disorder. *Autism Research 11,* 1, 95–109.

Lawrence, C. (2019) *Exploring Theory of Mind with Children on the Autism Spectrum: Two Sides to Every Story.* Banbury: Hinton House Publishers.

Chapter Fourteen

WHAT WE WISH TEACHERS KNEW ABOUT AUTISM

Autistic Voices

Jack Whitfield, Director of Autism Assemble, who works with autistic young people in the south-west of England, asked them what they would like teachers to be taught about autism.

'I wish teachers knew that...I get anxious. When I get anxious I need time out.' *Travis, autistic Year 10 student*

'I wish teachers knew that quiet, high functional children with autism need support too – and how desperately that child is waiting for that extra sentence directed just to him to tell him what to do. This reassurance releases so much anxiety.' *Zoe*

'I wish teachers knew that...attention-seeking behaviours, distraction, speaking out of turn, strong preferences for certain topics, or lack of interest [in certain topics], may be signs of autism rather than deliberate bad conduct.' *Keryx, autistic adult*

'I wish teachers knew that...I never mean to be offensive or rude. Anything I do is done without malice and it's important to me that people know that.' *Terry (female), autistic Year 11 student*

'I wish teachers knew that...we may not talk so often. We will still wish to learn if instructions are clear. People with autism/Asperger's aren't stupid, they learn differently.' *Gina, autistic young adult*

'I wish teachers knew...how to approach certain behaviour; not to shout as it upsets the individual; to understand an autistic person's mind and actions.' *Steven, autistic young adult working in theatre*

'I wish teachers knew that I'm not refusing to do a task to make you cross; I feel overwhelmed and don't know to express it. I wish I could organise the classroom so it makes sense to me. I want to make you proud of me but the pressure can be too much for me to manage emotionally. I know I'm "different" and it upsets me. I learn better when I can move freely, including rolling on the floor.' *Jack, aged 7*

'I wish teachers knew that...no one should be judged on their negative. Instead, work on them. Negative is just a positive that just needs to be worked on.' *Isaac, autistic young adult, performer and writer*

'I wish teachers knew that my child's autism doesn't mean he has bad behaviour – if autistic behaviours were dealt with appropriately they wouldn't be bad behaviour! I wish they knew that autism is part of my child and it will take him ages to learn new positive behaviours/ disciplines. I wish they knew that it hurts my child to hold a pencil for too long – it causes pain! I wish they knew that removing playtime for punishment doesn't work, as my child needs to run outside. I wish they knew that if you send my child to do a job, if he gets distracted he may be gone for ages and then forget what he was supposed to do. I wish they knew that he hates repetition and can get distracted. I wish they knew that high functioning autistic children still have lots of troubles and difficulties even though they are clever. I wish they knew that he needs constant help to support with keeping on track/target.' *Jenny*

'I wish teachers knew that...when I don't make eye contact I'm not ignoring them.' *John, autistic Year 11 student*

'I wish teachers knew that it has such a big impact when they have the training on how to support me better in the classroom but also enable me to learn strategies to manage difficult situations. I have had many teachers with lack of understanding making the classroom situation much more difficult. I wish teachers would know that I don't mean to be a hassle and make their life harder, but I really do try my best, just giving me small breaks, fidget resources and a lesson broken down in to small steps can go a long way. I wish teachers would just know how to understand what can help me succeed, looking at my strengths rather than my weaknesses.' *Freya*

'I would like teachers to understand how autistic people take things to heart often, and are driven by their hearts too. When I was at school the teacher would shout at the whole class, but I would always take it as my fault, even if I couldn't see what I had done wrong – it was compulsive. Now I support autistic students in schools myself, I'm trying to encourage teachers to engage with their special interests while working through the curriculum. I see autistic special interests as a sign that a lot of autistic kids have a pretty good impression of their respective destinies mapped out, and the real frustration comes in being asked to deviate from these dreams in academia when they can see the whole world around them orientates around adults working in very specific fields. If they know the specific field and interest they want to pursue already, why are they having to slow down to take in things they don't need or that don't make sense? That's why we need lessons made relevant to the individual, not the other way around.' *Jack Whitfield*

The Contributors

Dr Luke Beardon currently works as a senior lecturer in autism at the Institute of Education, Sheffield Hallam University. His interests extend to all things autism related and he has been working in varying capacities in the autism field since being a volunteer at a special school as a teenager. He holds an autism-related Doctorate and several autism professional awards, and has published widely on various autism-related topics.

Jo Cormack is a counsellor specialising in picky eating and feeding dynamics. She is the author of *Helping Children Develop a Positive Relationship with Food: A Practical Guide for Early Years Professionals* (Jessica Kingsley Publishers). Jo is a PhD candidate at Bishop Grosseteste University (BGU) researching how parents respond to childhood eating problems.

'Greg' (which is a pseudonym) is a newly qualified teacher of secondary geography. He qualified from BGU in 2018. Greg is autistic.

Jan Hargrave and Jo Tasker are relationship and sex education officers, working for Public Health, Lincolnshire County Council. Jan has a background in teenage pregnancy and healthy schools, and has a certificate of professional practice for PSHE, whilst Jo is a qualified counsellor for young people who has many years' experience of targeted youth support. She was instrumental in establishing the Lincolnshire Young Inspectors Project.

Sarah Howe is currently a senior lecturer in primary education at BGU. She has fulfilled safeguarding and child protection roles and responsibilities in early years settings and schools, and through her recent engagement in ITE programmes. She recognises the complexity and challenges that are associated with child neglect.

Dr Clare Lawrence is a senior lecturer in teacher development at BGU in Lincoln, where she is the Lincolnshire County Council Autism Champion for the BGU School of Teacher Development. Her primary research interest is in the mainstream education of autistic pupils, and she has written four previous books on the subject for Jessica Kingsley Publishers.

Steve McNichol is a senior lecturer at BGU where he leads the National Award for Special Educational Needs Co-ordination (NA-SENCO) and teaches on undergraduate and postgraduate initial teacher training courses. **Kersti Duncan** is a trainee teacher at BGU.

Lyndsay Muir is a senior lecturer in teacher education at BGU whose background is in applied drama and secondary school teaching. She has experience across all sectors and phases of education, as well as theatres, youth and community settings, creative businesses and training. Lyndsay's research interests include professional identity development with trainee teachers and applied theatre with trans people. Her TEDx talk 'Tea with Trans – what's on (and off) the menu' is available at https://m.youtube.com/watch?v=Y6CPVn9q3ao.

Shaun Thompson is a senior lecturer in primary education at BGU, leading on mathematics and special educational needs and inclusion across the PGCE course. Prior to this, he was a headteacher at a primary school and he has worked in mainstream and special education settings. His research focuses on supporting autistic pupils with mathematical problem solving and the use of visual representations. He has presented his work both nationally and internationally.

Helen Thornally is a senior lecturer at BGU teaching in teacher education with ITE and Masters students. Formerly a secondary school teacher in physical education and a head of sixth form, her educational career has allowed her to teach overseas. Her experience includes working with paralympic athletes, the All England Tennis Association and the schools dance company DDMIX established by Darcy Bussell. Her specialist interest is in extending the learners through appropriate adaptive pedagogies within the fields of health, exercise and sport within schools.

Jack Whitfield is Director of Autism Assemble, an upcoming social enterprise for vocational development, advocacy and empowerment in Devon and Cornwall.

Index